POSITIVELY OUTRAGEOUS SERVICE

"Scott delivers the inspiration of Fran Tarkington in the best-seller style of Ken Blanchard."
    —*Bruce Taffet, Senior Vice-President, United Artists Communications*

"A surprise to find that service can be fun!"
    —*Mike Nosil, Vice-President, Human Resources Department,*
La Quinta Motor Inns

"*Positively Outrageous Service* is a reflection of Scott's dynamic personality . . . a must read."
    —*Peter Lehy, Entertainment Accounts, Pepsi-Cola Company*

"An overwhelming success with our retailers."
    —*Jim Williams, Vice-President of Education,*
National Grocers Association

"Super . . . Customer service isn't an option; it's a prerequisite for survival."
    —*Glen R. Mielke, President/CEO, Builders Square (K Mart)*

"Loaded with examples of Outrageous Service . . . looks like a hit."
    —*Chuck Winans, Executive Vice-President,*
National Association of Concessionaires

POSITIVELY OUTRAGEOUS SERVICE
New and Easy Ways to Win Customers for Life

POSITIVELY OUTRAGEOUS SERVICE

NEW AND EASY WAYS TO WIN CUSTOMERS FOR LIFE

T. SCOTT GROSS

 MASTERMEDIA LIMITED
NEW YORK

MASTERMEDIA and colophon are registered trademarks
of MasterMedia Limited.

Library of Congress Cataloging-in-Publication Data
Gross, T. Scott.
      Positively outrageous service : new and easy ways
to win customers for life / T. Scott Gross.
      p.   cm.
      ISBN 0-942361-40-7 (pbk.)
      1. Customer service. I. Title.
HF5415.5.G76   1991
658.8'12—dc20   91-60812
                                                  CIP

Production services by Martin Cook Associates, Ltd.
Manufactured in the United States of America

10 9 8 7 6 5 4 3 2

A c k n o w l e d g m e n t s

There is no doubt in my mind that this book, like everything of consequence I have ever done, was co-authored by the best friend, partner, lover, critic, wife, and, if you believe in them, soulmate that a man could ever imagine.

Of course, special thanks go to others, like Vicki King, who taught me that a business book could be full of joy, and Ray Pelletier, who bought the first copy before it was even written. Both wonderful people have served this undeserving writer outrageously.

And special thanks must go to the hundreds of friends and strangers who contributed their ideas and stories. Also the wonderful, though sometimes vexing, people who have honored me by sharing their labor as my employees and have graced me with their common wisdom.

I am proud to say that my dad left me so many ideas and so much of his personal philosophy that I cannot look into a mirror without seeing him. Best of all—and every reader should be encouraged by this—this book is endorsed by Mom!

Still, if I listed a thousand names, the one at the very top of the list, in bold, capital letters, would have to be Melanie Gross. She read and typed almost every word of this book, questioned odd construction, and refused to admit fuzzy thinking.

Best of all, she loved me every day.

Contents

Preface

Positively Outrageous Service is a marketing strategy implemented one customer at a time. It is, in the fewest words possible, *participative service.*

Positively Outrageous Service isn't just something to be talked about in a book. It is something that I know *you* can do because I have done it. Anyone can practice the principles of P.O.S. and reap the benefits.

Positively Outrageous Service isn't necessarily a new idea. Most accurately, it is a reminder of old ideas that somehow got lost. It is the showmanship of a P. T. Barnum. It is the gracious hospitality of a Winn Schuller.

Positively Outrageous Service didn't self-create as a metaphysical "aha!" It evolved through my fortunate exposure to great lovers of customers who taught me that serving others is honorable and fun.

Enjoy!

POSITIVELY OUTRAGEOUS SERVICE
New and Easy Ways to Win
Customers for Life

1

WHAT IS POSITIVELY OUTRAGEOUS SERVICE... AND WHAT IS SIMPLY OUTRAGEOUS?

Positively Outrageous Service is the story you can't wait to tell. Everyone has a tale about a favorite restaurant, airline, or retail shop. Some of us have stories about manufacturers and distributors. But all of us have stories that are so good that we can't wait our turn. In these stories lie the secrets of retailing success, and in these pages those simple secrets will be told.

That is the good news. In other news, it is true that only a few will serve outrageously. Their stories of Positively Outrageous Service will be the success stories of the 90's. No one has a lock on either stories of the outrageous or the ability to deliver Positively Outrageous Service.

Positively Outrageous Service (P.O.S.) is unexpected service delivered at random. Sometimes the customer is invited to play along. P.O.S. is both out of the ordinary and out of proportion for the circumstance. It is a memorable event and is so unusual that the customer is compelled to tell others. P.O.S. creates lifetime customers.

The inner secret of P.O.S. is that it establishes a personal relationship between the server and the served.

We know that the shopping-fatigued customers of the 1990's will be looking for "an experience," just as they fervently scoured the malls looking for products in the 1980's. But P.O.S. has been around probably for centuries. And it should not be reserved for aging baby boomers. Indeed, every customer in every business or industry should be considered a prime target for P.O.S.

"Service," according to Webster, "is something done for others." It's something useful—I'll add desirable—provided *in addition to* goods purchased.

Positively Outrageous Service is something more. Here are some words that go well with Positively Outrageous Service: surprise, fun, unexpected, not necessary, playful, caring, entertaining, outrageous. Not all of these words will apply every time. Just understand that P.O.S. is out-of-the-ordinary service delivered in such a way that whenever you get into a discussion about your favorite restaurant, vacation, tailor, grocer, or—yes, friends, it is possible—government agency, this one positively outrageous experience is the one you relate to top all others.

IT'S UNEXPECTED

Robin Williams makes me laugh. Leonard Zittle prepares my taxes. No big deal! Williams is a comedian and Zittle is a tax accountant. Now Robin Williams, in my opinion, is one of the funniest comics in the business. And Leonard Zittle is an absolute master at the smoke and mirror of tax accounting. But neither laughing at Williams nor getting completed tax forms from Zittle is a surprise.

On the other hand, if at the end of a Robin Williams performance he announced that he would be available to answer tax questions . . . well, that would be as outrageous as having my accountant offer me a seat on a whoopee cushion. Positively Outrageous Service is unexpected service.

Robin Williams doesn't deliver P.O.S. even when he's being outrageous. Leonard Zittle doesn't deliver service that's outrageous even when his bills are!

Phil Romano got national attention when he created Fuddrucker's, a hamburger joint based on ideas that at the time were outrageous. When 99.9 percent of the industry used quick-frozen beef patties, and with a quarter pound being a more or less standard size, Romano opted to freshly prepare ⅓-pound patties in an on-premises butcher shop, visible through a large plate glass window to the customers as they waited in line.

Romano did more than paste "fresh" in bold letters on his menu. He elevated the concept of fresh to the science of P.O.S. In addition to such an unheard-of idea as an on-premises butcher shop, Romano installed an on-premises bakery. He even used stacked cases of fresh produce and cartons of bulk condiments to define the waiting lines that snaked through the restaurant! Want a cold beer? Pull one from the several tubs of ice water dotted around the dining room. Just remember to stop by the cashier station on your way out.

Those simple ideas were so novel that the courts later upheld the fact that they could be considered part of Fuddrucker's "trade dress" and that copy-cat operators were indeed stealing proprietary material. However, when Fuddrucker's expanded from a single off-the-beaten-path location to a multiunit operation, something happened. It was no longer a dining secret you could share with a co-worker or best friend. Fuddrucker's and their imitators were soon to be found almost everywhere.

The charm of helping yourself to tray upon tray of fresh sliced onions and tomatoes, pan after pan of crisp fresh lettuce, and an unlimited supply of bulk cheese sauce and condiments began, pardon the pun, to lose its freshness.

"Unexpected" is key to the definition of truly Positively Outrageous Service. It's the element of surprise and novelty that jolts the attention of the customer or patron and creates an experience that's memorable because it is so different from the expectation. Even if you are expecting the unexpected and don't know exactly *what* to expect, I guess you could call that the unexpected! Whew!

IT'S RANDOM

You can't give excellent service 100 percent of the time. Mistakes happen. That's a fact of life we cannot ignore. If you can't always give excellent service, how can you expect to always give Positively Outrageous Service? The better question may be, "Why would you want to?"

It may very well be that attempting to serve every guest, customer, or patron with P.O.S. would create an expectation that's nearly impossible to fulfill. Besides, there is something to be said for "keeping them guessing."

You want the customer to be able to depend on you for courteous, fast, accurate, complete service. But just once, or once in a while, serve them outrageously and they will be back expecting your standard good service but hoping perhaps for another chance to be served outrageously.

Once a customer has been served outrageously, he or she will project that experience into every future opportunity you have to serve them. In other words, one bout of P.O.S. will color every future occasion. You may be only providing your usual great service. But, to the customer, this experience will be colored by a fond memory of the previous Positively Outrageous Service.

Going above and beyond has merit, of course. But why create an expectation you can't possibly meet on a regular basis? In fact, there is a danger in attempting consistent P.O.S. Slip to mere excellence and the customer may feel cheated.

The Credit Union Executives Society invited me to speak on a week-long cruise through the Caribbean. In the Crow's Nest Lounge towering over the sea at the bow of the ship, my wife, Melanie, and I enjoyed consistently excellent service. Our Filipino steward made us feel more than welcome as each night we would watch the sunset over a glass of wine.

His name was Bito. On our second visit, Bito greeted us by name, and by the end of the cruise Bito was nearly family. We knew about his kids and his career, living aboard the beautiful New Holland luxury liner. So far, Bito's service was excellent.

On our last evening visit, Bito presented us with a hand-printed Dutch maiden's bonnet as a memento of our time together. It is beautiful.

What kind of tip do you think we left?

How would this story be different if I told you that *every* passenger received the same treatment? What if you patronized the lounge and did *not* receive one?

The same Phil Romano mentioned earlier opened an out-of-the-way Italian restaurant called Macaroni's. It's almost as if Phil was actually looking for a place to hide his operation. An independent, not inexpensive restaurant located in the boonies at least fifteen miles from downtown would seem destined for failure.

It didn't fail. The place is packed. Especially on Monday and Tuesday nights, the same nights that most restaurants struggle to keep their doors open.

Here's why. Other than the obvious fact that Macaroni's serves good food, Phil Romano had a gimmick based on the old Psych I principle that random reward begets regular behavior. In this case, the behavior is eating at Macaroni's on a Monday or Tuesday night!

Macaroni's seats close to 200, maybe more. But if you dined there on a Monday or Tuesday night and happened to get lucky, you—and every other customer in the joint—received a letter *instead of the bill.*

The letter stated that because the Macaroni concept was to make people feel like guests, it followed that it seemed awkward to charge guests for their good time. So once each month on a Monday or Tuesday, and always unannounced, everyone would eat free. The letter continued with ". . . Tonight is your lucky night." It went on to remind guests that the waitstaff was also working for free, so "please treat them generously." Almost as an aside, the diner was asked to "tell your friends about Macaroni's."

Would you call that P.O.S.? I do!

This practice continued until recently. Macaroni's is booming seven nights a week. Soon you'll be able to enjoy Macaroni's restaurants across the country. But for those of us who watched it grow and watched it go, the original will always be the best.

Eating free is definitely unexpected. By pulling this stunt at random, Romano not only managed to wow the customer, he was able to pack the house on nights when other restaurateurs were climbing the walls.

Let's take a marketing break and talk about Romano's strategy. First, his location is definitely out of the way. Worse, it's a single operation outside a major metropolitan area. Electronic media would be prohibitively expensive. Instead Romano blows his whole advertising budget by "comping" every ticket in the house once a month.

You could say that by picking up the tab for one out of eight (or nine) Mondays and Tuesdays in a month, he's managed a full house on what would normally be a dead night. And one out of eight amounts to a discount of only 12.5 percent. When you also figure that his waitstaff is working "off the clock," the discount is even less. Figure that his true costs, mostly for food and beverage, are much less than retail and you get an even clearer picture of Romano's bright idea.

Or look at it this way. One night comped out of thirty and you're down to a 3.3 percent ad budget, without considering actual costs. And look who he just put on his payroll—you! Testimonials are said to be one of the most effective forms of advertising. In one fell swoop, Romano gets a couple hundred tongues wagging, "You won't believe what happened to us last night . . . !" Effective? You bet!

What would the value of Romano's ploy be if it were always on a Monday instead of a Monday or a Tuesday? Why not just give everybody a 3.3 percent discount all the time? See? "Random" is the operating word.

Random rewards beget regular behavior. In this case, the behavior is going out to dinner at an out-of-the-way restaurant on a stay-at-home night just on the off chance that you may eat free. To his surprised customers, Phil Romano looks like a hero—a rich one.

IT INVITES THE CUSTOMERS TO PLAY

Some businesses have a built-in advantage when it comes to service; their customers are "in fun" when they arrive. Being "in fun" simply means showing up with the mind set to be loose and have a good time. People are much more likely to be "in fun" at the ballpark than at the dry cleaner's. But smart operators of any business look for opportunities to invite the customer to play.

We own three very different businesses, and you would be surprised at how willing our customers are to join in the fun once we start playing.

As a speaker at conferences and conventions, I find that people love to become part of the presentation. You can tease them unmercifully and they always bounce back asking for more. Audiences love opportunities to get involved physically, give their opinions, and share stories and ideas. It's surprising that more speakers don't take advantage of the natural feeling of being "in fun" while at a convention.

A favorite story happened while I was speaking at the beautiful Dana Point Resort in southern California. The audience became highly involved as I hammed it up and described the white chocolate macadamia nut cookie that we fresh-bake at our restaurant. The cookies are distributed at random as a little surprise for our customers. You can't buy 'em. It does no good to ever ask—they're free!

These cookies have helped build a second lunch run of high school students. The students don't know exactly when a delicious, hot, wonderful cookie will appear on their tray. So, not wanting to miss out, they've become regulars.

When our seminar broke for lunch, someone inquired about dessert. "We were hoping Scott would provide some of those delicious cookies" was the response.

Aha! An opportunity to serve up a healthy dose of P.O.S.! With a little help from the concierge, we arranged for the owner of the Chocolate Soldier, a nearby candy store, to deliver the closest substitute we could find: huge white chocolate and macadamia nut clusters.

7

Notice that not only was I serving outrageously but so was Denise Pardoen, the owner, who volunteered to make the delivery as soon as she closed the shop.

Just as my seminar was about to wrap up, in walked Denise, very sharply dressed and carrying a beautiful gold-foil box with bright red ribbon.

Unexpected, out of proportion, and highly involving, as my obviously pleased and surprised audience got a delicious dose of Positively Outrageous Service.

People love to hear their names and see themselves on videotape or in photos. I make it a practice to memorize key names and industry-related jargon before I speak so that I can better target the audience. Dropping a name, teasing a big shot, and telling theater folks about "trailers" and soft drink execs about "figals" are all good techniques for drawing the audience into the action.

In our video production business, using in-house "talent" creates an instant bond with the corporate audience. In this case, the easy route is usually the best route, because the result is a product that is eminently more believable. And almost anyone you ask is willing to jump in front of our cameras.

In our restaurant, it's amazing how "playing" with one customer often cues another customer spontaneously to join in the fun. Male or female, businessperson or day laborer, they all enjoy being invited to play.

Think about it. Doesn't being invited to play make you feel welcome? If being left out of the fun when the older kids went out to play hurt so much as a kid, doesn't it make sense that just being asked to participate can feel so good?

IT'S HIGHLY MEMORABLE BECAUSE I'M INVOLVED

Positively Outrageous Service doesn't have to be unexpected, out of proportion, and include an invitation to play. Hit two out of three and you're fine. P.O.S. will always be highly memorable.

There are thousands of messages competing for our attention.

The electronics and print media shout at us constantly. We trade television programming for at least some attention to commercials. The point is simple. If you want to be remembered, it's going to take something truly special to earn you a position in the customer's mind.

In an age when eating out is the rule rather than the exception, how do you grab top-of-mind position? With a dozen airlines serving the average large city, how do you earn customer loyalty?

One of the trends of the unfolding decade is that quality products will rule the marketplace. The days of cheap goods are nearing an end, if they are not already gone forever. With nearly every business capable of offering quality at a reasonable price, service will be *the* competitive difference.

In strictly manufacturing environments, the current thinking is that quality of design will be the competitive difference. Okay, let's not argue over the small details. Design is nothing more than how the product itself serves the customer. Product design can be surprisingly unique, surpass all expectations, and earn the admiration of customers who find the product easy or fun to use. Can we not say the exact same things about the design of the services we offer?

If service does indeed become the sole area of serious competition, what will be the major point of difference between you and the other guys? Positively Outrageous Service!

P.O.S. is out of proportion to the circumstance. That's one way that it becomes memorable.

Sitting in my dining room, I noticed a customer walk in with one of our printed bags. Now our specialty is carry *out*. I get nervous about carry-*in*!

Willie was working the counter, and I was confident that, whatever the problem, he would handle it promptly and courteously. Still, I listened.

It turned out that the gentleman had not received his correct order. Okay, not good. But not horrible either. After all, serving a hundred or so people in less than an hour is a difficult, sometimes confusing task. Most of the time we do it flawlessly. The gentleman was understanding and waited patiently while Willie apologized, quickly prepared the correct order, and apologized again. Good service, but not Positively Outrageous Service—yet.

I got up and approached my customer. "Hi! I'm Scott Gross. I own this restaurant and would like to apologize that we didn't get your order right the first time. Here's my card. Present it the next time you are in and lunch will be on me. And, Willie? Would you please add an ear of fresh corn on the cob, some creamy cole slaw, and one of our honey butter biscuits to the bag?"

"That's really not necessary," the customer said as he smiled. "I'm in here all the time, and you're always right on target. You're putting me into overwhelm!"

"That's the point," I said. "We are a little embarrassed that you would have to make two trips for one lunch, so we try to make at least the second one as pleasant as possible."

"Hi! I'm Steve. I'm the manager. I overheard your conversation but I was with another guest. Sorry I couldn't have handled your order myself. But I know Willie took good care of you!"

"Actually I've been more than taken care of. I hope you mess up again so I can get a repeat of this treatment. You can bet I'll tell the whole office about your good service."

It wasn't good service. It was Positively Outrageous Service. An unexpected, out-of-proportion response. And it turned a bad moment into a loyal customer and positive word of mouth.

Positively Outrageous Service is often so unusual that you feel compelled to talk about it.

Good friends of ours called excitedly to invite us for dinner at Little Mike's Ice House. Now that name does not conjure up visions of elegant surroundings and impeccable service. In fact, Little Mike's Ice House sounds exactly like the corner convenience store that it is. Who would expect that you could also get authentic northern Italian food and a family-style welcome in a place that sells beer by the quart and, from the outside at least, could hardly deserve a much higher status than "dive"?

In spite of food that turned out to be truly fabulous, my friends could talk only about the service. "Don't be shocked when you see the place," they said. "Wait until you've had a chance to sample the service before you make up your mind."

The neighborhood was so bad, I was afraid to leave the car unattended. We stepped around two sidewalk drunks drinking from paper bags to make our way to the oilcloth-covered tables corralled by folding metal chairs.

"Now can I make up my mind?"

"Not yet." They smiled.

Out from behind a wooden screen came a five-foot whirlwind of energy and hospitality. "Hi! I'm Anna. Are you hungry?"

"Yes, ma'am."

"Well, you'd better be. I don't like my food to sit on the plate. Do you like meatballs? Of course you do!" With a wink, she disappeared, only to return with a plate of softball-sized meatballs, steamy hot. You could smell them from ten feet. I couldn't wait.

"Here you go, honey." She beamed as she stabbed one with a fork and popped it into my mouth. "Once you taste some of Anna's cookin', I've got you hooked."

And she did. So what if it was served on paper plates? So what if you went to the fridge to get your own beer, soda, or wine (from bottles with screw-on caps)? At Anna's, you were made to feel at home, like family. And how many businesses make you feel like that?

"Use your bread to mop up the sauce. We don't use butter. That's what the sauce is for.

"Eat it or you'll wear it!"

And, of course, at the end of our first visit, we left as friends and bent low to proudly accept a motherly hug.

THEY LOVE TO FLY . . . AND IT SHOWS

We had been on the road for nearly a week. It was our anniversary eve, and we were left to wait for Delta's San Antonio flight to take us home. Melanie had a miserable cold. I was exhausted and just reporting the first sniffles of my turn in Hell. Happy Anniversary!

At the Delta counter, I made a feeble attempt at humor that was warmly returned. Explaining that we really were sick and tired, I asked the agent to check our boarding passes for frequent-flyer registration.

Just before boarding, an announcement summoned me to the counter. "Mr. Gross, if you will trade me your boarding passes, you and your sweetie can go ahead and board." With that, she handed me two boarding passes that put us into first class.

Delta is known for good service, which I believe stems from Delta's legendary "people first" style of management. But our upgrade to first class qualifies for Positively Outrageous Service status. Why? It was random, unexpected, and highly involved us, and was so memorable that we've become Delta customers for life.

As the door was about to close and the jetway removed, a gentle tap on the shoulder got my attention. "Mr. Gross," said a tall, handsomely uniformed gate agent. "I'm sorry I missed you at the gate. I just wanted to wish you and Mrs. Gross a happy anniversary and hope she's feeling better soon. Thanks for flying with us tonight."

There was an eclipse that night, and we strained to watch the darkening moon as it danced from cloud to cloud. A memorable sight. That was our fourteenth anniversary, and it's safe to say that on at least some of the preceding thirteen anniversaries, we were enjoying much more exotic and seemingly more memorable venues than the inside of an L-1011, first class cabin notwithstanding. But I'll tell you this. Because of the Positively Outrageous Service of a couple of heads-up Delta gate agents, this is the only anniversary for which I can recall such wonderful service.

Needless to say, for this one act of unexpected kindness, whenever I'm confronted with a choice of air carriers, Delta gets the nod. A no-cost incident of P.O.S. purchased a lot of positive, valuable word of mouth.

PICTURE THIS

Harry Boyd owns a camera store. He also owns my patronage for life.

I enjoy photography. My wife is a dark-eyed beauty. So take me to a beautiful tropical island without a camera and you might as well shoot me! I wouldn't give a plugged nickel to look at scenery unless it's through a lens.

Three days before a trip to Oahu, Kauai, and Maui, my telephoto lens died a slow and agonizing death. Harry Boyd confirmed the fact.

"No problem, Harry. Sell me another."

"Big problem, Scott. I don't have one, and it's doubtful there's another like it, new or used, within a thousand miles."

Big problem for me. No problem for Harry Boyd.

Harry promised me a new lens in time for Hawaii or I could take his personal camera gear. Not a small offer from a man I had just met.

But Harry Boyd came through. The new lens he ordered, delivered via overnight express, arrived just in time. Nice story. Good service, too. Maybe not truly Outrageous Service.

Explaining that my camera was more than a little outdated and that I would no doubt be in to purchase new equipment in the near future, Harry said he didn't have the heart to charge me full price. Harry discounted the list price by 25 percent, paid the freight charges, and earned himself one solid-gold customer for life.

That was seven years ago, and since that day I haven't darkened the door of another camera store. Harry Boyd and crew have since given me consistently excellent service plus one instance of more Positively Outrageous Service, just enough to keep me guessing.

Unexpected, random, customer invited to play, and so memorable that compelling word of mouth and possible customer-for-life status occurs. That's Positively Outrageous Service.

Whenever I'm asked to recommend a great place to eat, whenever I choose an airline, whenever I need to buy film or camera equipment, there's no avoiding thought of Macaroni's, Little Mike's, Delta Airlines, or Harry Boyd. All have served me outrageously and, in so doing, have captured me as a customer for life.

Positively Outrageous Service is rare, but it doesn't have to be. Stick around and I'll show you how to bring P.O.S. to your business, too!

13

P.O.S. MARKETING

Positively Outrageous Service is a marketing tool. It is participative service in action as you market in the new-old way, one customer at a time.

Retailers won't miss the intended hidden meaning behind P.O.S. It also stands for Point of Sale. The principles of Positively Outrageous Service apply nicely to more than the organized activity of what has come to be known in a too-small circle of retailers as event selling. We'll apply the principles of Positively Outrageous Service to the broader strategy of P.O.S. Marketing.

Although some remarkably large corporations have begun to discover the advantages of one-on-one marketing, P.O.S. is primarily the tool of the small business. P.O.S. is marketing with the rifle of one-on-one promotion and service rather than the shotgun of now-traditional mass media and "take a number, please" service.

WHAT IS SIMPLY OUTRAGEOUS?

Bill Oncken was one of the few management gurus to ever say anything of practical value to the everyday manager. Often, when lecturing, Bill would coax the audience to define comedy, only to observe that the definition of comedy is also the definition of tragedy. Comedy or tragedy—it's only a matter of perspective.

"One man's comedy is another man's tragedy," Bill would intone before showing the group how that same idea of perspective applied to management.

Subtle differences also determine whether your service will be Positively Outrageous Service or merely outrageous. Perhaps even outrageously poor service.

Think about the worst service that you have ever experienced. Think about the airline flight that turned into a first-class disaster, or the evening on the town that could have been a movie titled *My Dinner in Hell.* Think about the bank that promised fast, convenient service and then left you to rot in their drive-through lane.

Your worst service memories were random and unexpected. You were highly involved, perhaps to the point of shouting and threatening to sue. And, of course, the event was highly memorable, easily earning its place in your repertoire of "the worst service I ever had" stories.

Sounds just like the definition of P.O.S., doesn't it? It is.

Just as delightful P.O.S. earns a business a permanent position in the mind of the customer, its antimatter cousin also earns permanent mental residency. The difference, of course, is a matter of sign—positive or negative. While P.O.S. in its positive sense creates lifetime customers, service that is merely outrageous—outrageously poor—turns once-positive opportunities into an unending saga of negative word of mouth.

Worse even than just not returning, customers who have been treated outrageously will with little provocation gladly repeat the tale of their mistreatment in graphic detail.

A few years ago, we were drawn on impulse to a local Jeep dealer. An ad featured in the morning newspaper listed one Jeep Cherokee at a super price. Off we went—just to look, of course.

It was a beauty. Not wanting to miss a once-in-a-lifetime deal, we willingly allowed ourselves to be marched into the sales manager's office to sign on the dotted line.

"Sorry," he said. "It looks like another customer is in the next office and he also wants that Jeep. It's yours, though, if you insist."

"I'm easy," I said. "Give me as good a deal on another Jeep and let him have it."

"Let me have it" would have more accurately described what actually took place. First there was the surprise of several hundred dollars for "dealer make-ready." Then the shock of discovering that my mint-condition trade-in was actually a clunker on its last legs, which, as a favor, the dealer would take off my hands.

"Sorry, we just can't offer much. We'll have to pull some strings to get one of our wholesalers to take it."

But the final straw came later.

Driving home in my beautiful, new-smelling Jeep, discovering unexpected bells and whistles decidedly dented the gnawing feeling that just maybe I had been had. But what the heck. Then my wife spoke.

"You won't believe what that sales manager said," she offered coyly.

"What?"

"Well, first promise that you won't go back down there."

"What?"

"Well, when you got up to go to the water fountain, he said I am a beautiful woman . . ."

"Well, you are. I can handle the fact that other men find you attractive."

". . . and then he said that if I wasn't being treated like a beautiful woman should be, I should give him a call."

"What?!"

I have not bought a new vehicle since. There's a good chance that I never will again. But every time someone has asked how I like my Jeep, I tell them this story.

Random and unexpected. The customer highly involved. Definitely highly memorable. A non–customer service of negative word of mouth for life.

Merchants in our small town are often criticized for being a bit pricey. Many times the criticism is justified.

Walking into a local office supply store, we discovered that the markers we use in our restaurant were considerably higher-priced than what we were accustomed to paying in nearby, much more competitive San Antonio. We opted to purchase only a few to get us by until our next trip to the city.

Our mistake was mentioning to the owner that there was a big difference in price between her store and out-of-town suppliers.

"I know you," she said, hands on wide hips as she blocked our exit. "You own the restaurant over at the mall."

"Yes, ma'am, we do."

"Well, rents are higher in this town, and it costs more to do business here. You ought to know that. You should be supportive of the community that makes your living. There's something you should think about!"

With that, she let us pass out of the store and away from the stares of surprised shoppers.

She was right. There was something to think about, and think about it we did. Before we made it to the car, we had decided that under no circumstances would she ever have an opportunity to berate us in public again. Nor would she be selling us any more overpriced office supplies.

Unexpected and random. An out-of-proportion response, and the customer intimately involved in a highly memorable way. Strong word of mouth and a lifetime buying decision were the result.

Positively Outrageous Service or simply outrageous—the blade cuts both ways. Two sides of the proverbial coin: Heads you win, tails you lose.

2

SAM WALTON'S KILLING ME! OR WHY P.O.S. IS *THE* COMPETITIVE ADVANTAGE

Look at the longhorn steer. When the grass gets short around the water hole, he goes farther out.

—Great-Grandpa Rhyne

It was a beautiful spring evening as we drove deserted streets past a dozen or more small businesses, some closed early for the evening, some closed forever. At the far end of town, only Wal-Mart could boast a full parking lot. And the scene could have been Anywhere, U.S.A. If it's not a picture of your town, just wait.

The discounters have brought variety and quality at low prices to small-town America. Sam Walton can't be held responsible for the resulting deaths of scores of Main Streets. It is true, though, that many would like to lay the blame squarely at his feet.

Sam just had a good idea—first. About half of his detractors must secretly wish that they had had the same idea—first. That plus the guts to do something with it.

Wal-Mart has created quite a stir with its impact on small-town America. But that's only because it's easier to spot trends and connect cause with effect in communities that rarely stretch more than a mile or two border to border. Even though small-town America has become our laboratory for studying the impact of discounters, it would be foolish to even hint that the same things don't happen in our largest cities.

There are no cities. Just clusters of small towns. For most retailers, if the edge of the world were suddenly moved to within a two-mile radius of their store, it would be up to CNN to let them know, because the impact at the cash register would be negligible.

If it hadn't been Sam Walton who spotted the need for variety, quality, and value, it would have been someone else who would be labeled the despot of Main Street. Even in small towns, individual tragedy is too easily overlooked when the community is apparently benefiting from a trend that for the first time brings toasters and microwaves to lower- and middle-class homes.

Besides, a toaster is easier to notice once it's sitting on your counter than old man Smith's now-closed variety store. And wasn't he about to retire anyway?

In the larger sense, the Smiths of Anytown have been edged out by the quick-witted marketing savvy of Sam Walton and others. But it hasn't really been a case of sophisticated city slicker M.B.A.'s knocking off well-meaning but ill-equipped small business people. Too often the little guy has cried foul when the truth could be more easily found in the mirror.

It's not fair to call the casualties of retailing cry babies. Most fought bravely and didn't quit until well after the battle was lost. But they *are* guilty of fighting poorly.

The following is an article from a small-town Texas newspaper. The names have been changed "just because."

UNFAVORABLE CONDITIONS CITED AS REASON FOR SELLING

Charlie Smith owned and operated a local business for fifteen years but was *forced* to sell out to a major chain for various reasons that revolve around what he feels were unfavorable economic conditions.

Smith's opened in 1973 and was experiencing 12 to 24 percent increases every year up to 1986, Smith explained.

He felt the business was a successful one at that point.

In 1985 the small business had its best year ever, with sales totals exceeding $750,000.

"Gross profits were good and net profits were good," Smith explained.

This banner year and the twelve previous years gave Smith the idea of expanding and investing in an attempt to instigate a growth pattern.

It was at this point that trouble began, according to Smith.

He went to the bank and borrowed money to invest in his business. Remodeling was done and new equipment was added to the existing stock.

"We had no reason to think that the economy would fall apart in 1986," he added.

Smith researched before committing to such a large investment. He found that the interest rate was favorable, unemployment was down, the Gross National Product was stable, and inflation was down.

"We could only assume, because of sales, we would do well because of the stats and our previous sales," continued Smith.

He said the Anytown Area Chamber of Commerce might be at fault in a sense.

"They play a numbers game," he explained. "It's their job to make the numbers look good regardless of what they actually are.

"I am not denying the fact that the figures are factual the way they present them. However, they play with the numbers until they appear positive.

"I know because I have played the game," he said, alluding to the time that he spent on the board of directors for the Chamber.

Another large factor for the loss of Smith's was the opening of Wal-Mart four years ago.

Smith explained that Wal-Mart carries "quick-moving items" that appeal to many buyers.

In an attempt to keep people buying locally, Smith kept many of the slower-moving items in stock.

"Things people need very seldom," Smith explained.

The "quick-moving items" are the "cream of the crop," according to Smith. And once he started losing his normal sales, he was forced to stop stocking the slower-moving items.

"In most areas we were always competitive with Wal-Mart and our service ability helped us," continued Smith.

After surviving K Mart's invasion into the area, it was difficult to come out on top with Wal-Mart, he said.

"There is only a certain amount of available monies in the area, and when you are forced to split them three ways in an economically trying time, you will not win," Smith explained.

It was early in 1987 that Smith and his family realized that they were not going to make it.

He tried once again to borrow money from a financial institution in an effort to stay on his feet until the "depression" was over, he said.

"We had adjusted out all variables in our outgoing money," Smith said. "All businesses have to look to lending institutions when times are bad.

"When the lending institutions will no longer support you in your efforts to regain stability, this is what happens."

Smith sold his business to his franchisor.

"I sold out under duress and paid everybody I owed," he said. Smith said he would go back into business tomorrow if he had private investors and did not have to borrow from an Anytown lending institution.

Smith is a nice man, the kind of man you would want for a neighbor or mayor or favorite uncle. But, nice or not, look again at the article and see who he thinks is to blame. He blames K Mart, Wal-Mart, the economy, and finally the local bank for not supporting an obviously failing business.

At least he had the good grace not to blame his neighbors for shopping with the competition. In that respect, Smith is an exception. In small towns everywhere, consumers are being berated for not keeping their dollars local. Running into a friend at a nearby big-city mall is like meeting your preacher at a topless bar. You both hope you won't be recognized, and if a meeting can't be avoided you both blubber out some lame excuse for existing!

Smith was a brave soldier and a dead one. He didn't understand the uncomplicated concepts behind the Four-Walls Marketing Theory. Neither did the protagonist of the painted window story.

THE PAINTED WINDOW STORY

The intersection was just west of Boston. Too far from town to be called a suburb but too close to be considered a part of Boston. Some 300 feet from the corner sat an A & W Root Beer Restaurant. You remember A & W, don't you?

At one time the A & W family consisted of nearly 2,500 mostly ma-and-pa operations scattered across America, with a smattering of foreign operations. A & W is the restaurant chain that should have been McDonald's. They were there first, often in the best location, and frequently without competition.

But A & W either wouldn't or couldn't change. They failed to recognize and respond to a changing consumer. Today A & W is but a shell of its former self.

It was the lunch hour when the young A & W field rep walked into the restaurant. He had noticed that weeds were growing through the cracks in the parking lot and that the light standards had begun to rust. Inside, the few tables that had been occupied by the sparse lunch crowd were still dirty. Crew members were out of uniform. A radio was blaring.

The owner, known for his love of fishing, was resting feet up, tying a fishing lure. He stared out the window at the new, sparkling clean, and very busy McDonald's that had been built smack on the corner.

Without shifting his gaze, the owner said, "That damned McDonald's is killing me! Ever since they opened that damned place, my sales have gone straight into the dumper! If you think you're going to continue collecting royalties from me, you'd better get off your backside and help me out!"

"No problem," replied the youngster.

With that he quietly let himself out of the office. In about twenty minutes, he returned carrying a small brown bag.

"Here. This might be just what you need to turn the corner."

"What's this for?" asked the owner as he removed a very small can of black paint and a small, inexpensive brush. "What am I supposed to do with this?"

"Paint that window black," risked the field rep, "and I think you'll have less trouble with McDonald's. Judging from the looks of your parking lot, dining room, and employees, my guess is that McDonald's has done more than attract the attention of your customers. It looks like they attracted your attention as well.

"Looks to me as if they're paying more attention to your customers than you are," he continued.

"Get out!" was the owner's reply.

The field man left. But it was the owner who got out. Permanently.

FOUR-WALLS MARKETING

The idea isn't new. Neither is the terminology. Unfortunately, for all of our sophistication, we have somehow forgotten that ultimately our marketing strategies live or die within our own four walls.

In simpler times, when our competitors were unable to reach out and entice our customers with an electronic message, people understood intuitively that taking care of business meant taking care of the customer. And that, of course, meant making certain that whatever transpired within our own four walls had to be perfect.

When populations are spread thin, and competitors are far apart, marketing loses its meaning. It just isn't convenient to travel long distances for small savings on life's necessities. Marketing makes sense only when your competitor locates within easy traveling distance of your customers. It makes even more sense when your competition sets up shop right next door.

Still, marketing only begets trial. It is the daily, one-on-one activity that occurs inside your own four walls that creates compelling word of mouth and repeat business.

Few businesses can survive by serving a customer only once and then looking for another new customer to take his or her place. Four-Walls Marketing is whatever you do that turns customers into friends. In the 1990's successful Four-Walls Marketing can mean a revival of the new-old techniques of serving outrageously.

23

BIG FISH, LITTLE FISH

The big fish do eat little fish. That's the way it has always been. Still, there are little fish.

Even the big fish worry constantly about some bigger fish swimming around some dark corner. So if even the big fish aren't safe, what's a little guy to do?

The problem isn't what *size* fish you are. It's what *kind* of fish you are that counts.

Little fish don't get eaten simply because they are little. It's more a matter of being in the wrong place at the wrong time.

Today's giant discounters are worried about "category killers," mega-operations that focus tightly on a single product category such as toys or office supplies. It's not unusual for the sales of entire product categories to be decimated when a "category killer" decides to open in close proximity to a discounter.

Category killers have such enormous buying power that they can purchase in truckload quantities for factory-direct delivery. Even the Wal-Marts, K Marts, Sears, and others don't usually have the volume to individually require truckload orders from a single manufacturer.

Truly, in retail, when it comes to being price competitive, the only thing that counts is distribution. Every time you hear the sound of air brakes at someone's dock, listen closely for the sound of a price going up.

The point is this: If you're a little fish, don't even dream of beating 'em on price.

Service—Outrageous Service—is the advantage that belongs to the littlest, most responsive fish. Little fish that serve outrageously swim rings around the competition.

THE ANSWER, MY FRIENDS, IS BLOWING IN THE TRENDS

The little guy can't compete on price, and discounters are devouring the American market. That's hardly encouragement to the millions of businesses in America with ten or fewer employees. Or is it?

Actually, several trends in America are working to the distinct advantage of those small businesses with the foresight to act rather than react. All of these trends put a premium on participative service.

If Positively Outrageous Service is the epitome of participative service, then those businesses that serve outrageously will enjoy a distinct competitive advantage.

TREND ADVANTAGE #1: DECLINING LEISURE

By the year 2000, three-fourths of American families will be dual-income families. With two breadwinners at work, most American families are enjoying a high standard of living. In fact, the average American has twice as much buying power today as in 1952. By 2000, three-fourths of American families will have two wage earners, making for a society that's long on dollars but short on the time in which to spend them.

In fact, by 1985 the average work week had already reached forty-nine hours, causing available leisure time to decrease by a full one-third in little more than a decade.

Because time is at such a premium for many Americans—and what could be more personally involving than one's time?—unexpectedly fast service will be received as Positively Outrageous Service, a gift almost of life itself. After a customer has decided to purchase, we are working on his time.

Small businesses often have a distinct speed-of-service advantage over their larger, slower-moving competitors. As Stanley Davis says in *Future Perfect,* "Time is a small business strategy and resource."

If speed of service is a major advantage, when it comes to leisure, quality of service will be the competitive edge. With fewer leisure hours to spare, Americans will increasingly be on the lookout for high-impact experiences. The businessperson who can bring entertainment value to even such mundane chores as groceries will be king.

The small businessperson has considerably more creative free-

dom and control over the operation. But beware! A creative entre-
preneurial spirit occupying a position of corporate power can set
even large organizations buzzing.

Crazy Ed and Hot French Bread

All I wanted was a box of cereal, a can of fruit cocktail, and a
newspaper. She wanted me to have French bread. Not really ordinary French bread but hot, fresh, would-you-like-to-smell-it French
bread. She pushed a cart draped with a red-and-white checkered
cloth up the cereal aisle. I thought she was on her way to the deli.
Nope. She was hawking, actually hawking, French bread in the
aisles of the supermarket.

Just as she docked her cart next to mine and squeezed off a quick
smile, the P.A. system exploded.

"Goo-oo-ood afternoon, Albertson's shoppers! Come on down to
the deli and pick a pack of Crazy Ed's deli-fresh pizza. You can take
'n' bake or pick it up hot to go right here in our deli. So come on
over and see why Crazy Ed's pizza is the right choice for lunch!"

No waiting. Personal service. Great entertainment value.

Even grocery shopping can be a Positively Outrageous Service
experience!

When leisure time is limited, consumers will be drawn to where
the entertainment is the best, even if it's to be found in unexpected
places.

TREND ADVANTAGE #2: QUALITY BECOMES THE RULE

In the Old West, the Colt .45 was known as the great equalizer. Big
man or small man, a large-slug revolver tended to blur the differences. As we approach the turn of the century, the computer has
helped eliminate many differences in product quality. Today, almost
every complicated manufactured product is a high-quality product.
The choice is no longer between premium quality and imported

junk. Today it's more a matter of differences in color, style, and features.

Not only will quality be the rule, quality products will be affordable. Technology, high and low, has resulted in prices on some items actually declining in real dollars. Think about electric drills, TV's, VCR's, even frying chickens! This means that, more than ever, service will be *the* point of difference.

Dr. William Wilsted of Ernst & Young has studied how various issues of quality impact the buying decision. According to Wilsted, there are three "dimensions of quality" that drive purchase decisions:

- Effective: Does the product perform as advertised?
- Responsive: Will the product be delivered on time?
- Personal: How does the customer feel about the purchase?

Wilsted's own descriptions are a bit more academic, but we'll report his numbers exactly. According to Wilsted, while the provider perceives that the personal relationship with the customer weighs in at only 10 percent of the buying decision, the customer gives it a weight of 70 percent!

In an age when the aspects of quality that can be measured by the physical sciences will be ever more standardized, the social interaction of service will acquire increasing significance.

One additional factor of quality straddles the border between product effectiveness and the personal relationship between buyer and seller. That is the dimension of design. A product that works according to design is not necessarily a product that is designed according to the work. Only those companies with the closest relationship with the customer will be able to design products that most accurately target customer needs.

TREND ADVANTAGE #3:
BUYING HABITS ARE POLARIZING

Okay, so service is indeed the competitive advantage. But what if I don't want service? After all, there are some products that are more like commodities. Take toilet paper as an example. Most consumers don't particularly need, or even want, service with their t.p. Give it to me soft and give it to me cheap.

As the decade unfolds, the American middle class is growing while the richest and poorest segments of society are shrinking. Yet at the same time our buying habits are tending to the extremes. More and more consumers are discovering that many product purchases don't require service. For such commodity-like products as gasoline, toilet paper, and laundry detergent, American consumers are flocking to the discounters.

The amazing thing is that the money we Americans save on the necessities is going right into the purchase of luxuries. It is not at all uncommon to see a luxury automobile being fueled at a self-serve filling station. Look in the parking lots of the growing number of wholesale-to-the-public or so-called warehouse stores. You'll see luxury cars belonging to owners who don't feel at all uncomfortable shopping in a warehouse for commodities before reporting to the beauty salon for a manicure and facial.

It's important to notice that even budget-conscious, do-it-yourself types are not settling for sub-par products. They expect the quality. It's in distribution that they are willing to compromise. "Okay, I'll pack it myself. I'll buy it in bulk. Just give it to me cheap and make sure it's the good stuff."

For the heads-up entrepreneur, it's important to realize that dollars saved at the discounters are waiting to fall into the open hands of businesses offering personal-touch, boutique-style services.

TREND ADVANTAGE #4: NAISBITT WAS RIGHT—HIGH TECH/HIGH TOUCH

Nearly a decade ago, John Naisbitt identified a trend that he called High Tech/High Touch. It is the tendency to balance the tensions of a hard-edged high-tech world with the soft, calming amenities of high-touch endeavors.

More fast-food meals meant more gourmet meals cooked at home. More commuting through rush hour meant more bicycling on country roads. This is a trend that both continues and plays directly to the outrageous server.

High-techies will be easy picking for businesses that will surprise them with individual service and the opportunity to become personally involved with the selection, production, and serving of their purchases.

By the year 2000, over 20 percent of Americans will work at home. This will include the operators of more than 20 million home-based businesses. For the most part, these workers will be high-techies working with their computers, fax machines, and modems. When they do get out, they'll be hungry for more than lunch. They'll want to see a friendly face. They'll want, perhaps expect, a little conversation.

Because Positively Outrageous Service is the most involving, touching kind of service, the trends favor those businesses that serve outrageously.

One bitingly cold Denver morning, I set off into the snow in search of a battery for my microphone. Just around the corner, I found a 7-Eleven, my battery, and this wonderful story.

Her name was Roberta. At least that was what her name tag announced. Her total attention belonged to a tall, elderly gentleman who had placed his purchases on her counter. He stood as straight as possible, adjusted his collar and scarf, and extended a gnarled hand.

Roberta slipped the handle of the plastic bag onto his wrist and waited for a second age-spotted hand to find its way to hers. She warmed his hands as tenderly as I've ever witnessed, then, calling him by name, smiled and said, "Be careful. I want to see you again tomorrow."

"Not what I expect at a 7-Eleven," I said. "How come the special treatment? Is he related?"

"He's my customer," she said, a short phrase that explained it all. Then she tossed her hair and smiled. "Oh, thank heaven for 7-Eleven."

And today she was right.

TREND ADVANTAGE #5: DESIRE FOR CUSTOMIZATION

In Henry Ford's day, it was "any color you want as long as it's black." Today, thanks to computer-assisted manufacturing, it is becoming increasingly cost effective to customize. You can still achieve the economies of mass production and custom-produce on the same line. To a computer-directed laser cutting device, it doesn't matter or even slow the system to order item number 38,615 a quarter-inch larger.

When things can be custom-produced at will, then there will be a rising demand for custom service as well. "What do you mean you can build me a car to my personal dimensions but you can only deliver it between nine and five?"

And custom service can even apply to a commodity.

"How do you customize a commodity? You standardize the commodity and customize the services that surround it" (Stanley Davis, *Future Perfect*).

Watch Out, McDonald's!

"Hello. Nonnie's Cafe 27!"

"Hi! What do you have for dessert tonight?"

"All we have left is fresh pecan pie."

"Sounds good to me, but my wife isn't nuts about pecan pie. What's for tomorrow?"

"What would you like?"

TREND ADVANTAGE #6:
AN AGING CONSUMER

"I didn't realize that we are living in an age when service is the exception until I took my daughter shopping. I couldn't find what I wanted and so I said, 'Let's ask the clerk.' My daughter looked at me with embarrassment and said, 'Oh, Mother!' I realized then that there is a whole generation out there that has come to feel that they are not entitled to excellent service" (Linda Finlin, San Antonio, Texas).

Kids don't have much expectation of service. If this was 1965, this book on service wouldn't have been written. Quite simply, books and seminars and videotapes on service exist only because their moment in history has finally arrived.

In the 60's you could pretty much open a restaurant, theater, or youth-oriented retail operation and stand back and count your dollars. Don't try it today unless you know exactly what you are doing.

Those kids that hung out in front of the skating rink or miniature golf course in the 60's are today's largest market in terms of both numbers and disposable income. Pay attention to those boomers. If you can predict the tastes of the baby boom generation, you can see the retailing future.

If the kids aren't yet interested in service, their parents, on those schizophrenic off days when they're not filling the Mercedes with bulk t.p. at the Wholesale Club, more than compensate as they demand ever-higher levels of personal service. And why not? The *Wall Street Journal* says they are tired. The specific malady? Shopping fatigue.

"Research published by the *Wall Street Journal* last fall [1989] revealed that many Americans plan to curtail their acquisitiveness. Three-quarters of those surveyed said they had fulfilled most, if not all, of their material needs. The *Journal* called this attitude 'shopping fatigue.' The majority of Americans may now want to clear their closets and shop for new experiences, not new merchandise" (Francesca Turchiano, *American Demographics*).

"The over-45 crowd used to hate spending money and trying new things. Now they're spending their money on experiences rather than assets. What was once a great market for Cadillacs is now becoming a great market for travel" (Stanley Buchin, senior vice-president, Temple, Buchin, Sloane).

Whether an aging population is good news or bad news is entirely up to you. It seems clear that if you are selling experience, such as travel or education, you may be in the right place at the right time. But even if your product is Cadillacs, you will still do well if you make buying and owning a Cadillac an experience rather than a simple purchase.

According to Ken Dychtwald in his landmark book *Age Wave*, Americans over fifty represent only 25 percent of the population but control 70 percent of the total net worth of U.S. households "and account for a whopping 40 percent of total consumer demand." Dychtwald called these people seasoned consumers: "Even though they pay attention to price, they are more willing than younger people to pay for quality and service that will make their purchase cost-effective in the long run."

So businesses of the 90's are presented with a consumer who has the money to buy but already owns the world. Actually, the world is the only thing the 90's consumer doesn't own, and it will be the travel agents who, in effect, "sell the world" who can expect to really clean up.

In fact, those monoliths of retailing, regional shopping malls, will quite possibly be among the first visible casualties of an aging, changing consumer base. Think about it. Are shopping malls designed for people in a hurry? Are stores located in the middle of a mile-long enclosed mall conveniently located? Are most malls havens of high touch in a high-tech world? No, no, and no.

Turchiano says, "Shopping centers are a mega industry on the brink of a mega decline. As many as 20 percent of the regional shopping centers now operating in the United States will close by 2000 and the declines will continue into the 21st century. The survivors will pay close attention to the expectations of their customers. The doomed will stick to business as usual."

And just what will those customers expect? Why, an experience, of course! And better that it be Outrageous!

You may find the kids eating at McDonald's, but the folks with the dollars and the highest frequency of eating out will be at Lambert's Cafe in Sikeston, Missouri.

Jane White of Houston, Texas, told this story: "Mother and I were driving to Houston from Chicago. In Sikeston, we started having trouble with the car. We were forced to spend the night at the local Holiday Inn because it was late and the dealer couldn't get a mechanic to look at the car until sometime the next day.

"The wonderful couple who managed the Holiday Inn told us, 'If you're not going to do anything else in Sikeston, you've got to eat lunch at Lambert's.' I had seen a sign that said 'Lambert's Cafe— Home of the Throwed Roll' and had remarked to Mother, 'What in the heck is a throwed roll?'

"Well, this couple said we'd have to find out on our own, and they even volunteered to drop us off at Lambert's. At 11:00 A.M., there was already a line a half block long. I thought, 'Boy! This place is really popular.'

"We started talking to other people in line and found out that they were from all over. One lady told us that people came from as far as Chicago just to eat at Lambert's because it's the greatest place in the whole world, 'because if you want a roll, they throw it at you!' Then the waitresses follow with buckets of hot molasses and other things to put on your roll to snack on while you're waiting.

"Well, I asked the waitress how all this got started, and she said, 'Why don't you ask Mr. Lambert?' She brought Mr. Lambert to our table, and he was the nicest gentleman you could meet. He asked what we were doing in Sikeston. When we told him about the car, he immediately got up, called the dealer, and made sure our car was next in line.

"Then he ordered coconut cream pie for us. We told him we were full, but he said you're never too full for his coconut cream pie. And besides, it was his treat.

"In fact, he paid our entire bill! When we insisted on paying the check, Mr. Lambert said, 'Anytime I've been in trouble, somebody has helped me. Maybe when you're in Houston you'll tell somebody about Lambert's Cafe. That's how I get my business."

And she did.

You can buy coconut cream pie cheaper at the discount house. It is frozen. Coconut cream pie tastes better at Lambert's Cafe. It's worth the trip.

Random and unexpected;

Out of proportion to the circumstance; and

The customer is invited to play, resulting in compelling word of mouth and lifetime buying decisions.

Catch!

HOW TO FIND OUT WHAT CUSTOMERS REALLY WANT

The cake was grand. Smothered in cherry topping and wrapped in a thick cream frosting, it was a birthday surprise. When the office finally cleared, one little piece was left to carry home to my wife.

Not surprising, when it was her birthday she asked for a cake just like the one they had served at my office celebration. Problem was it had been home-baked by a temporary worker, whom we couldn't locate.

No problem. I'll call a bakery, describe the cake, and who will be the wiser?

"Hello. I'd like to order a yellow sheet cake with cherry topping, kind of like what you would find in a cherry pie. And can you put a cream frosting on the sides and perhaps in a lattice pattern across the top?"

"I'm sorry, we don't have a cake like that."

"Well, it's fine with me if we don't get it exact. But could you try, please?"

"It's not in our book."

"Yes, ma'am, I understand that. I was just hoping that I could describe the cake and you would bake one for me."

34

"I wouldn't know what to charge."

"Well, charge me whatever you think is fair and then add five dollars for your trouble, just to make sure you come out all right."

"I can't. If it's not in our book, we can't bake it."

"Do you bake yellow sheet cakes?"

"Yes, that's a number four."

"Do you bake cherry pies?"

"Yes, that's a number seventeen."

"Great! Bake me a yellow sheet cake and a cherry pie, but before you put them into boxes, scoop the pie filling onto the cake."

"That's not in our book, sir."

True story.

Here's one with a happy ending at McGuffey's Restaurants in Asheville, North Carolina:

A family entered a McGuffey's with a very unhappy child in tow. It seems that the kiddo had his heart set on eating at McDonald's. When the news of the unhappy diner reached the kitchen manager, an employee was immediately dispatched to a nearby McDonald's, and within minutes a Big Mac was delivered to the surprised child.

Serving the customer what he wants may not be found in everyone's book. But at McGuffey's it's on page one!

The whole of business is finding a need and filling it. And you can't fill a need unless you know about it. Any business that doesn't have a system for customer feedback is a solution looking for a problem.

In our own business, our number-one rule is: "Always try to say yes to a customer. Say no when it's for their own good."

In *Customers for Life,* Carl Sewell puts it like this: "When the customer asks, the answer is always yes. Period."

Pretty firm position, but only if you know what the customer wants. You would think that customers would come right out and tell you what they want. It seems so obvious. In fact, customers don't always tell you what they want, particularly if what they have is a complaint. Complaints are requests to get it right, to keep your promise.

Every sale carries with it a promise. With service the promise is often only implied.

For $14.95 you get a fourteen-ounce T-bone cooked to order with choice of potato, fresh vegetables, and a garden salad. Appetizers, drinks, and desserts are not included. Read the menu, dummy! It's all there in black and white!

On the other hand, convenient parking, clean restrooms, comfortable, smoke-free surroundings, pleasant greetings, and efficient, friendly service—that's all implied. Part of the cost, of course!

The same is true for any other purchase. A new computer comes with power cord, monitor, manual, and system software. It's all listed on the box. But can I call you if there's a problem? How many times? Will you be able to assist? Will you *want* to assist? All this is implied.

Funny thing about service: It's a major portion of product cost but rarely mentioned on the packaging.

You would think that customers cheated out of their service would complain. According to the U.S. Office of Consumer Affairs, between 37 and 45 percent of consumers who are unhappy with service do not complain. They go elsewhere.

They may go elsewhere, but they never forget. And when they remember you, it's always with the kind of word of mouth that causes you to die a thousand deaths: once from embarrassment and 999 times at the cash register as would-be customers get the message. They join the one dissatisfied customer as they "vote with their feet and cross the street."

We mentioned earlier that the definition of Positively Outrageous Service is more than an outline of the best service you ever experienced. It also defines your worst service experience. When you talk with people about a P.O.S. experience, they are usually champing at the bit for you to finish so they can tell a story of their own. This is also true when it's a story of outrageously poor service.

Outrageously poor service, like its upbeat cousin Positively Outrageous Service, is random and unexpected; it is out of proportion to the circumstance; and it highly involves the customer. And it, too, creates compelling word of mouth and lifetime buying decisions.

For this reason, every business needs a customer service feedback system. Call it damage control, if you wish, or just call it enlightened business acumen. But have one you must.

According to an article by Patricia Sellers in *Fortune Magazine,* there is a surprising payoff for those companies that make a science of listening to the customer: "When they make their customers happy, they make their employees happy, too. Contented workers make for better-served customers. And there is also mounting evidence that improvement in customer satisfaction leads directly to higher employee retention."

In the end, nearly everyone is a customer. Particularly in a tight labor market, a business hopes to market its package of wages, benefits, and working conditions to the employee. After all, what is retention anyway other than an expression of employees' feelings about the value they receive in return for their investment of time and energy?

As long as we're being enlightened, we may as well include your suppliers in the same package. Suppliers stop at many other doors before and after you. They can provide marketing and product development insights, price breaks, and delivery and billing flexibility. And some even provide their customers with management development. Treated properly, a supplier can be a major asset.

Wise is he who listens, for in the end we all are customers. In the end, we all vote with our pocketbooks and with our efforts. And in the end it is he who listens who includes us, empowers us, and wins our loyalty.

MBWA—TOM PETERS SAID IT!

Can't you see some starch-shirted manager wringing his hands while pondering the question "How can we find out what customers really want?" Think about it. There he sits in a plush office somewhere deep in the halls of the Puzzle Palace hoping for divine intervention with a problem the receptionist could solve between calls. Ask them!

Tom Peters helped popularize the concept of MBWA—Management By Walking Around. Such an obvious concept that it's embarrassing. Still, we get so hung up on technology, psychology, and demography that we forget that the best way to find out what your customers want is to *ask*.

James (Buddy) Parker used to say that comfortable offices and pagers were two things that effective managers would never need. "Gives them an excuse to be someplace they aren't supposed to be," he said on many occasions.

If your job was to serve the customers or support those who did, then Buddy couldn't figure what use could an office be. It should, he figured, be just large enough to accommodate a safe, one chair, and an adding machine. More than that and you are cheating the shareholders by squandering their assets, and cheating the customers by denying them your attention.

Pagers fell into Buddy's same dark category. If you are supposed to be in the store, then why do you need a pager? If you can't be easily found, then you are out of place. Period.

Whether it's Peters or Parker, the place for management is with the customer, guest, patron, or member. And the higher up the ladder, the *more* visible you should be. After all, beyond a quality product, what can we give the customer? Quality service, of course! What is not so obvious is that a major component of service is status.

I'D RATHER MEET A DUMB OWNER . . .

Stephen Michaelides, editor of *Restaurant Business,* once made an interesting observation: A customer would rather meet a dumb owner than a sharp manager. What he meant was that since status is such an important component of customer service, then by the very fact that the owner—make that OWNER—takes a personal interest in the guest (customer), more status is conferred.

He did not say that it's okay to hire stupid managers! What is true is that the higher an individual resides in the corporate hierarchy, the greater the impact of direct customer contact.

People revel in their stories about being greeted or treated by the owner: "The owner came out and introduced herself." "The owner took us on a private tour of the facility."

Excellent or perhaps just good service delivered by the owner, president, or grand pooh-bah takes on outrageous proportions simply because such people add their personal status to the event.

WOO!

Donald Clifton, president and CEO of Selection Research, Inc., offers an interesting customer-based method of evaluating your business. Clifton's measuring sticks are awareness, preference, frequency, and relationship extension.

Awareness is expressed as the percentage of your potential market that is aware of your operation. Aware customers or potential customers are those who know your location and perhaps your hours of operation, and have a general knowledge of your products and services.

Preference is expressed as the percentage of your market base that, given a choice, would prefer your product or service to that of the competition.

Here's where Clifton's measurements get interesting. Frequency is the number of visits or purchases per month or year or whatever. Relationship extension is reflected in the percentage of your customers who feel that they are recognized as individuals. Being called by name is probably the most important indicator, but it's not the only one. "Good morning, Mrs. Tate" may be perfect, but "Hi! I haven't seen you in a while" certainly runs a close second.

What is interesting is how frequency and relationship extension relate. Quite simply, the more you extend a personal relationship to your customers, the more likely it will be that they will increase their patronage. Theoretically, it's possible to double your sales without adding a single new customer. All that must be done is to make your current customers feel so good about doing business with you that they come in twice as often.

Impossible? Not at all! In our own operation last week, sales were up 82.6 percent over the same week last year, with only a minor increase in sales per transaction. Most of that increase was due to higher customer counts. And the town is not one iota larger or richer. Something changed, and that something happened within our own four walls. It's called better service.

Relationship extension is Don Clifton's term. I call it Feel Good.

Feel Good. That's just another name for status. And who can give the customer the most status? Why, the dumb owner, of course!

In most businesses it's not possible for the owner to meet and greet every customer. Most customers don't expect such attention. They do appreciate the owner's presence. Having the owner on hand usually conveys a certain sense of security that the product or service will be done right. And if there is a problem, the owner is at least available.

One of Clifton's other terms is "woo." For those instances when a customer must be handled by an employee, Clifton says the magic word is "woo." Woo is that touchy-feely personality trait that allows employees to reach out and, in a matter of a few seconds, extend a little Feel Good to the customer. Woo, unfortunately, is not an easily trainable talent. You either have it or you don't.

Employees with woo are the best customer feedback system possible. Woo people listen and respond instantly to the customer's needs. They make thousands of operational adjustments every day as they ride the ebb and flow of individual customers' emotional needs.

The trends are unmistakable. Success in the 90's will belong to those who are best at honoring the oldest traditions of customer service.

Listen to your customers. Give them exactly what they want, any way they want it. And invite them in to participate in their own service.

This will be the new-old way of succeeding, an announcement of a return to the days when the customer was both a friend and neighbor. Now there's a concept that's positively outrageous!

3

TALES OF THE OUTRAGEOUS

The manager was armed with a gun—a spray gun, that is—and a roll of paper towels. He attacked the dirty windshield the instant the driver stopped at the menu board in the drive-through. He and the unseen owner, who was working the speaker from the inside, carried on a playful banter while coaxing an order from the customer, who was by now laughing hysterically.

At the pickup window, the still-laughing driver said, "I've never had *that* happen before. When are you going to do the inside of the windows?"

The owner smiled. "I'm not sure. Tomorrow we're doing hairstyling, and Saturday we'll be trying our hand at dentistry!"

And the word spread.

And it was fun!

Ken Blanchard calls it "stepping out of the box." Jack Welch is said to believe in "change before you have to." Bill Oncken preached the gospel of "standing out" as being even more important than being outstanding.

Whatever you call it, serving outrageously almost always involves an element of risk. As it turns out, "risk" is one of the best words in the dictionary. It has semantic kinship with more than a dozen words that each pack a punch as powerful as dynamite.

"Risk" leads to "adventure," "gamble," and "luck." "Risk" leads to "audacious" and "daring." Just look at the wonderful words and the feelings they represent.

"Adventure: an exciting undertaking."

Here's a fabulous relative—"adventurer." It cuts to the very heart of capitalism. "A person who tries to become rich by dubious schemes." Entrepreneurs love it. Bankers cringe at the thought. But what the heck—if bankers were risk-takers, they would be running their own businesses instead of pontificating about how you should run yours!

And look at another risk-related word: "audacious—daring or impudent." Positively Outrageous promotions are often both daring and impudent as they fly in the face of conventional wisdom.

"Risqué" is a kissing cousin to risk. It means "very close to being improper."

"Risk," though, is word enough to describe the conditions of being positively outrageous in your marketing and service. "Risk: the chance of running into danger; to expose to possible loss or damage."

Does this all sound too far out, too dangerous? Then go work for someone else. Stay safe in your office. The entrepreneurs of this world have created millions of job opportunities. They've made millions. And, because it's the very nature of the beast, they've lost millions. But win, lose, or draw, the entrepreneurs, the risk-takers, always are standing when the bell signals the start of another round.

Besides, psychologists tell us that a number-one indicator of a healthy mind is the willingness to take a reasonable risk. Think about it. The crazies are curled up in a fetal position. The risk-takers are doubled over, but it's from laughter as they play out their hand in a game as big as life itself.

"The first-class mind is an independent mind. It is never totally for hire. The intellectual does not automatically agree with the boss, and he would not be of much use if he did" (Hedley Donovan, former editor-in-chief, Time, Inc.).

The following tales of the outrageous all share a common trait. They are the stories of risk-takers who champion the art of playing out of bounds. They are the stories of the offbeat, who look at the conventional wisdom and draw unconventional conclusions. They are the stories of people who are "at play" twenty-four hours a day.

SMARTFOODS

I built a team of pyromaniacs.
—Ken Meyers

Read the small print on the front of Smartfoods Popcorn and you'll get the idea that you are holding an extraordinary product. "Famous since 1985" instantly attacks the idea that only longtime products can be excellent. The corner copy that announces the precise number of kernels popped is the second tickle of irreverence.

Still, the striking black bag adorned with simple graphics and accented with power words like "ultimate," "bursting," "premium," and "totally natural" completes the image of a fun company that is clearly committed to producing a quality product.

Turn the bag over and the message intensifies. Read the left panel and you are certain that president Ken Meyers and his band of merry men and women are totally committed—and they should be!

Open the bag and try some. Just a little. (I dare you!)

Okay. Now that you've eaten the whole thing, may we continue?

Imagine the difficulty Ken Meyers and crew must have encountered trying to break into the crowded, highly competitive snack foods business. They didn't have a mega-corporation to tap for marketing dollars and expertise. It's a good thing they didn't. Supported by mega-bucks and conventional wisdom, Smartfoods Popcorn would have never been a smart food.

The packaging is all wrong. Everybody knows that popcorn should be packed in clear bags that tear straight to the bottom the instant you attempt to open them. And, oh, yes! Commercially produced popcorn is supposed to be orange. Who wants white popcorn? It turns out that, once tasted, everybody does!

Right from the beginning, poor old Ken Meyers took the contrarian approach. He used a black opaque foil bag, air-popped corn, no artificial colors or flavors, and white (imagine that!) cheddar cheese. Then, in a fit of insanity, he decided to brag about it on the back of that ridiculous bag.

HOW WE DON'T MAKE OUR POPCORN

Unlike some naughty companies who do mean and nasty things to their popcorn, we treat our kernels with the love and respect that real food deserves. We DON'T drown our kernels in preservatives. That wouldn't be fair . . . they can't swim.

We DON'T make our kernels wear funny-looking colors. Let's face it, it's embarrassing! Besides, bright orange cheese isn't normal.

As for artificial flavor, we DON'T let our kernels roll around in that stuff. It spoils the natural taste of delicious popcorn.

What we DO is combine fresh, air-popped popcorn with the best, lightest corn oil and the most delicious WHITE cheddar cheese seasoning to create a totally natural, wholesome and delightful product.

Poor Ken Meyers. It took him all of five whole years to grow Smartfoods from zero to $50,000,000! Imagine what he could have accomplished with a couple of drums of Day-Glo orange food color.

Like so many really great concepts, Ken Meyers's version of guerrilla marketing did not stem from genius. Necessity once again became a mother. Ken talks about the enormous sense of pride he felt when he was finally able to put together a $100,000 marketing budget. Walking out of the ad agency office, Ken wore an entirely different emotion.

"They just sort of laughed and said they could get me four weeks of radio in Boston and they didn't care what I did with the remaining $13,000."

I asked him how Smartfoods would have been different if he had started with millions.

"If we had had millions of dollars at our disposal, we would not have reinvented the wheel."

Ken Meyers's brand of marketing was "born of necessity. It best demonstrates and presents our passion and religion."

I didn't ask Ken exactly what he meant by "religion," but I don't think he meant religion in the traditional sense. Besides, Ken Meyers doesn't seem to possess a single serious bone in his body. He's the kind of guy who would probably take the collection plate and pass it along—filled with Smartfoods Popcorn.

So Ken Meyers turned away from—or was turned away by—conventional marketing and developed a style that is best characterized as:

- Different
- Low-budget
- Personal

As Ed McMahon would say, "How different is it?"

Would you consider larger-than-life Smartfoods bags snow-skiing to be different? How about marathon runners dressed in huge Smartfoods bags? Does a parade of dirt bikes towing Smartfoods billboards register on the bizarre scale?

Emily Fagundo does public relations and advertising for the Meyers maniacs. One of her favorites was a series of billboards that featured the tag line "Smartfoods—You can't get it off your mind." One of the illustrations showed a very elderly gentleman marrying a very young, beautiful woman. Her thought balloon said, "$'s." His was filled with a bag of Smartfoods Popcorn.

Emily says that the folks in the Smartfoods marketing department are all marketing geniuses. (And that they pay her well to spread the rumor!)

But it's true that you can't talk to anyone at Smartfoods without wondering just what exactly is in their thought balloons.

One ad campaign featured the world's largest coupon on a billboard. "Bring this to your grocery and save big on Smartfoods," read the copy. The coupon amount: $500 off. You guessed it! An enterprising housewife recognized a deal when she saw one and, armed with an X-Acto knife, managed to peel the coupon off the billboard and haul it to her grocer. Naturally, Smartfoods paid off: $500 worth of Smartfoods Popcorn!

Smartfoods marketing is low-budget. After his rebuff by the ad agency, Ken refused to give up. He still needed to grow his business. Only now he would look for ways that didn't require so much financial muscle. Instead he turned on the creativity.

45

According to Ken, "Our most perfect marketing tool turned out to be the package . . . and the product itself." With that, he began a series of outrageous promotions that put Smartfoods Popcorn into the hands (er, mouths?) of potential customers at a cost of mere peanuts—make that popcorn.

Meyers takes his product personally, and that is exactly his approach to marketing. He believes that the objective of his person-to-person guerrilla-style marketing is good old-fashioned word of mouth. His job is to "spark a few" so that they in turn "will spark many more."

Campaigns that are low on budget must be high on creative energy. To accomplish all this high-energy, product-to-customer marketing, Ken says, "I built a team of pyromaniacs. They are the great painters of this art."

Ken's "painters of the art" set out to turn Smartfoods Popcorn into a cult product by taking the product to the people. The playful approach gave Smartfoods entry into consumers' minds. As one popcorn-suited hireling so aptly put it, "They don't see us as advertising. They see us as a moving festival." In other words, Ken's borderline bizarre promos so involved the consumer that Smartfoods came to be viewed as part of the fun.

Emily Fagundo tells how wearing a Smartfoods tee-shirt into a supermarket is a sure conversation starter.

"Where did you get that shirt?" is the usual question. She is awarded near-celebrity status when she explains that she got it at work. Emily says, "People don't feel like they are being pitched by Smartfoods promos because the events are just that—events."

Ken Meyers describes Smartfoods's guerrilla marketing strategy as the "highly visible, larger-than-life marketing of a promise and then making good on that promise." Perhaps it would be just as instructive to take a close look at this popcorn miracle and walk away chanting "different, low-budget, personal." In one form or another, these three words describe promotions that are positively outrageous.

(P.S. The last time we talked by phone, just as we were about to hang up Ken asked me my waist size. "Waist size?" I asked. "Why do you want to know that?" "So I can send you some Smartfoods boxer shorts! Everybody does tee-shirts!")

DECORAH, IOWA

We draw from a wide area, and that doesn't happen by accident.
> —Mike Donahey, executive director,
> Decorah Chamber of Commerce

The central business district of Decorah should have died a long time ago. Storefronts should be boarded up and sidewalks rolled up. Discovering that the town is not just alive but actually doing well is a surprise. The town is a contradiction, and, as Mike Donahey might say, that doesn't happen by accident.

Decorah was characterized by *Adweek's Marketing Week* as a town that "turned the tables on Wal-Mart." When you discover exactly how they managed to do what some would call impossible, it's enough to make you throw marketing theory to the wind.

Talking to Dave Rambo and Jerry Aulwes, two downtown Decorah merchants, is like talking to Smartfoods's Ken Meyers in slow motion. Therein lies the secret of Decorah.

Positively Outrageous Service is alive and well in downtown Decorah. For sure, you're not likely to encounter Positively Outrageous Service of the borderline bizarre variety. But we never claimed that really grand service had to be loud and flashy.

We do stick to the notion that *different, low-budget,* and *personal* are the power principles of marketing in the 90's. And, as much as it might appear that the central business district of a small Iowa town belongs to another place in time, principles of management and marketing tend to be like wide or narrow ties: They'll come back in style if you wait.

If you need to talk to a Decorah merchant, just call the store. Chances are they'll personally pick up the phone after a ring or two. But, if not, you'll find that they haven't strayed too far or that they won't be gone for long. Dave Rambo is usually first to the phone, just as he's first to admit that the Wal-Marts of the world have "probably made better merchants out of us."

Dave says that in other towns people will tell you "I don't go downtown. There isn't anything there." Not true in Decorah, where you will find four or five nice dress shops, three hardware stores, and several nice shoe stores. Not exactly what you would expect in a town of 8,350, which probably includes cats, dogs, and attorneys.

Decorah's strategy, organized in part by the Chamber of Commerce but more by the Decorah Betterment Association, is to offer customers a wider selection in the central business district. According to Dave, "Wal-Mart likes to be the only place in town with a good selection. If they can do that, they've got you beat. Downtown, we've managed to offer a wide selection."

At Jerry Aulwes's Coast-to-Coast Hardware, selection is an important strategy, but so is pricing. Decorah may be a little country town, but its merchants are as up to date as anywhere.

Jerry says, "When Wal-Mart came in, we changed a few of our lines. They want rapid inventory turns at low prices." Rather than compete head to head on a hundred or so loss-leader items, Aulwes and others carry the next-higher-quality product line. Not only does this avoid the issue of direct price comparison, it gives the customer more choices, and those choices are on higher-quality items.

As for the other items, Jerry and friends are very competitive. Variable pricing strategy is considered by some to be a technique reserved only for sophisticated retailers. It's alive and well in Decorah. "Customers don't remember the prices on slow-moving items. Their [Wal-Mart's] prices are very high compared to ours on slow items. People don't think to check these prices." (Decorah merchants don't let their customers miss the difference.)

Downtown Decorah gives customers something different, and, while they've managed to attract consumers on a relatively low budget, they did recognize the need to provide landscaping, ample parking, and attractive storefronts. It was the focus of the Decorah Betterment Association to provide these shopping amenities in an effort to keep a step ahead of the malls.

Rather than roll over and play dead as larger competitors moved into the area, the central business district merchants continued to advertise and market their businesses.

Aulwes gives this advice to merchants faced with new, aggressive outside competition:

- Don't panic. According to Aulwes, some merchants get so scared, they quit business before the competition arrives.
- Watch your prices. Make changes before the competitor arrives. Pick up a list of "price-conscious" items.
- Go to "best-price" policy on key items, but leave others at regular mark-up.

In spite of sophisticated pricing strategies, no one had any illusions that small merchants could compete seriously on the issue of price. The small-town merchants of Decorah decided to stick to their game to force new competition to meet them on their terms and press fully the home-team advantage.

The Decorah merchants decided to get personal.

"We give a lot better service," says Aulwes. "They claim service and they try. But we do it better."

At Aulwes's Coast-to-Coast, you can get your bicycle repaired, window screens replaced, and guns reworked. Believe it or not, there's even a bridal registry. One of Jerry's clerks accompanies the prospective bride (and/or groom) on a tour of the store and lists each appliance or hand tool. Customers love it because it virtually eliminates duplication and exchanges.

Aulwes loves it, too. Personal service and wide selection are the reasons he cites for the need to move into a new building, more than doubling his space only two years after competition should have shut his doors.

I knew instantly that Decorah had won on the issue of personal service when I asked Aulwes how many of his customers he knew by name. "My wild guess would be 40 percent, but it may be more. But then again, I've been on the City Council, and that could make a difference."

Knowing 40 percent of your customers by name is a decided

competitive advantage. Knowing 25 percent is considered outstanding. Imagine what it must be like to shop at Rambo's Pharmacy. Dave estimated that he knew about 80 percent of his customers by name until his wife, standing nearby, said, "I wouldn't think 80 percent. You know about all of them!"

Rambo, who has been in Decorah a week longer than always, probably does know everybody. He likes to tell about his first job, where his boss advised him that the most important thing to a person is his name. Rambo took that lesson to heart and, at the end of the first year, knew almost all of his customers by name.

It was a simple lesson that Rambo never forgot. He knows that he must offer even his most long-term customers a reason for shopping at Rambo Value-Rite Pharmacy.

"I don't have to beat Wal-Mart, but I do have to be fairly close. They use a system of loss leaders. In fact, on one high-priced, brand-name drug, a customer told me I was twenty dollars less than Wall-Mart." Dave laughs and says, "I had to recheck my book pretty quick on that one. But it does show that they have items where they jab it to them."

Dave's full answer to price competition is personal service. "We charge drugs. We deliver. I know them, their parents and their kids. It helps a lot, especially when the bloom is off the rose elsewhere. I like my customers to say 'They know me when I walk into Rambo Pharmacy.' "

TUESDAY MORNING

It's not just a day of the week.

Different, low-budget, and personal. That perfectly describes Tuesday Morning, the Dallas-based deep-discount retailer. When Tuesday Morning sends four-color sale announcements to its millions of devoted customers, you can hear the roar of an equal number of Mercedeses and Cadillacs as they converge on the company's low-budget, definitely secondary, perhaps even tertiary locations.

The concept that drives Tuesday Morning's success is simple: high-quality gift merchandise at deep, deep discounts. Discounts in the 50 to 80 percent range are standard.

Corporate purchasing agents scour the market for end-of-run, close-out, returned, and remainder merchandise, and typically cut deals at 10 percent of regular retail. At those low product costs, even an 80 percent discount from retail leaves a comfortable margin.

Most discounts are around 50 percent. Still, in spite of low prices compared to retail, Tuesday Morning merchandise is neither inexpensive nor "cheap." You may be able to find bed linens or wine goblets at a lower price elsewhere, but not of Tuesday Morning's quality.

The company specializes in "designer"-label, top-of-the-line merchandise. There are no irregular or mystery brands to be found on Tuesday Morning's shelves.

But there is a definite air of mystery about shopping at Tuesday Morning, an air that serves to heighten the experience and create a feeling of exclusivity. Tuesday Morning stores are not open year-round. The outlets are open for business only four times a year, in February/March, May/June, August/September, and November/December. Notice that these dates correspond neatly to the retail industry's peak selling seasons.

What makes Tuesday Morning radically different is that store locations are like the merchandise . . . deeply discounted. You won't find fancy fixtures at Tuesday Morning. You'll be lucky to find the store!

But find the stores they do. Well-off customers, tipped off via direct mail three days in advance of media advertising, flock to the out-of-the-way warehouse settings to haul off treasures by the carload. Service is nonexistent. It is the eccentricity of the concept that turns the chic moneyed into well-dressed wrestlers as they wade into the crowd, arms and credit cards swinging.

These early-bird customers are proud to be on the Tuesday Morning mailing list. It is not unlike being a member of an exclusive club, a head-start rush at a cavernous store full of high-quality bargains. What's more, you never know exactly what to expect.

This event-selling atmosphere creates intense customer devotion.

51

Tuesday Morning customers have been known to drive for hours and postpone major engagements. One (it is reputed) had her husband's open-heart surgery delayed two days so it wouldn't interfere! Weddings and showers are scheduled to take advantage of sales periods. Some customers show up in chauffeured limos and van pools, knowing that parking will be at a premium.

Different, low-budget, and personal is the hallmark of Tuesday Morning's positively outrageous brand of promotion. The merchandise is a surprise, discounts are out of proportion to your expectations, and select customers are personally invited to play. Tuesday Morning sales events create such excitement among devoted customers that compelling word of mouth makes Tuesday Morning the best unkept secret in town!

BERRY HARDWARE COMPANY

Mission: *We want our company to make a positive impact in our world and in our community through service to others and service to ourselves and our families.*
—*Tom Guyton*

They aren't praised at elaborate company banquets. Nor do they fly from coast to coast on lavish corporate jets. Most of the time they answer their own telephone. But that is only when they're not busy helping to put up stock or visiting with customers. And you won't find them having cocktails with clients, although they may stop for a quick glass of iced tea at the local diner. Even then they keep one eye on the clock, not wanting to be too long from the store.

These are America's quiet heroes. More likely to contribute to the Little League or deliver food baskets at Christmas, they seek a lower profile, having made a choice to serve not the masses but the individual.

Georgetown is a quiet, city-sized village located smack on the old Chisholm Trail, a short drive north of Austin, Texas. Just as the town's founders were pioneers of the American West, Georgetown's leading citizens of today are pioneering America's tomorrow. One of these modern heroes is Tom Guyton, owner of Berry Hardware Company.

In 1977, when Tom, a former groundwater engineer with a degree in finance, walked into Berry Hardware Company, it was love at first sight. Located on the west side of the town square, the 135-year-old company was housed in a building with eighteen-foot ceilings and bare wooden floors. Six weeks later, Berry Hardware Company belonged to Tom Guyton.

"Mr. Berry had turned down other potential buyers because they had the 'wrong attitude.' When I asked, 'Can this business be bought?' he looked at me carefully and then replied, 'Maybe.' " Even in 1977, Berry Hardware Company was a throwback to times long since past.

Tom bought the business on the condition that he retain the store's honorary manager, an eighty-five-year-old gentleman who arrived each morning to occupy his post, a red metal lawn chair just inside the front door.

In those days, many items were stored in bins rather than mer-chandised on shelves or hooks. Customers would enter the store and wait until a clerk could escort them to the appropriate bin and extract the product. "You never knew what you were going to pull out of those bins," said Tom.

Tom, who collects antique clocks and often drives a 1919 Model T truck, thought he had purchased a simple business and expected to spend his days chatting with customers. He had visions of playing checkers with friends and living a life destined to be immortalized on a *Saturday Evening Post* cover. Tom was dead wrong. "I never worked so hard in my life!"

Worse, in 1977 downtown Georgetown had not benefited from a new coat of paint or a new idea in too many years. Shortly after coming to grips with the reality of the hardware business, Tom began to realize that he and his fellow merchants couldn't continue to survive in a world that had ceased to exist.

Most of the upstairs windows along the town square were boarded up. Several storefronts were vacant, and, worse, downtown merchants eyed each other with suspicion. Maybe it was Tom, maybe it was just an idea whose time had come. Whatever the cause, around 1978 the downtown merchants began to realize that the real competition had not yet arrived. That year, talk began in earnest of banding together not to save the idea of a town but to save each other.

By 1981 Georgetown merchants were organized and talking. And Tom had already pushed sales at Berry Hardware to nearly triple their 1978 sales. Still, Tom knew serious competition could—and would—threaten further progress. "We didn't know if it would be Wal-Mart or K Mart. We just knew they were coming."

In 1981 Tom created the first strategic plan in the company's now 139-year history. It came not a moment too soon.

In 1982 several major events occurred that would shape the future of the Guyton family, Berry Hardware Company, and the dozens of merchants whose lifelines were so firmly anchored to the old town square. That year the downtown building owners and merchants embarked on a multi-million-dollar plan to restore the town to its original, circa-1890 glory.

Berry Hardware Company moved to larger quarters at 212 West 7th Street, into what the Historic Association describes as "a poured concrete expression of early 20th-century industrial design." Occupying this relatively new (1938) former Pontiac/De Soto automobile dealership, Berry Hardware Company was ready for the third major event of the year.

In 1984 the merchants of Georgetown realized one of their greatest fears. The inevitable happened. Wal-Mart announced it would build on a large-acreage tract out on the interstate, where it most surely would intercept customers motoring in from Georgetown's growing suburbs.

The announcement turned out to be a gift, because it would be several years before Wal-Mart would actually open its doors. Tom Guyton had time to continue whipping Berry Hardware Company into competitive shape.

Capitalizing on the principles of different, low-budget, and personal, Tom and his staff set out to position Berry Hardware Company as the place to go for selection, quality, and personal service. He also wanted to cement his relationship with the community.

Berry Hardware Company became further involved with community work and was soon known as a caring community leader.

Tom studied the competition and extended his hours. "We knew that the competition would be open on Sundays. In this business, Sunday sales come directly from sales made during the week. But if the competition is open on Sundays and a customer needs hardware, then we know people would be forced to go to them if we didn't offer an alternative. If you knock on our glass, we'll open the door. You can even call us at home." Try that with a discount chain!

Tom studied his competition and moved his cashier right up to the front door. "We don't just say, 'Hi!' like the discounters." Instead, Berry Hardware Company employees are trained to offer customers advice on their projects. Tom says that one of his biggest jobs is training employees how to help customers on a variety of do-it-yourself projects. He also made certain that the customer-to-staff ratio was low enough that customers who need help can get help.

After studying his competition, Tom made certain he had as little merchandise overlap as possible. He also prepared to match or at least get close to Wal-Mart's low prices on key items.

Right after he purchased the company, Tom affiliated with the Ace Hardware Company, which gave him the purchasing power of a large buying group and helped him remain competitive. On "blind items," those on which customers are not likely to be price-aware, Tom refuses to overextend his mark-up. "Customers are not stupid. If you can hang on the first few months, they'll figure out that discounters don't give them either the discount or selection they expect."

Tom's approach was low-budget—fair prices, good selection, plenty of service—except for one minor indulgence, a twenty-by-thirty-eight-foot American flag. "We wanted the world to know that something special is going on in Georgetown." The flag flies from a monster-sized pole planted right in front of the store.

"Man, I saw that flag and I wanted it. It was the most impulsive thing I've ever done. I decided to put it up and then ask forgiveness" from the planning and zoning board.

Stop anywhere on the square and ask a resident for directions to Berry Hardware Company. Chances are they'll just point to the flag. Tom had a veterans' group formally install the flag as a choir sang "God Bless America." Tom says it was quite an event.

Personal service is a hallmark of Berry Hardware Company, where you can charge hardware to a thirty-day account, have a pipe threaded on an ancient machine, make a five-cent copy, or send a fifty-cent fax. Seems logical in a place where booting up the computer nets you a happy rendition of the *William Tell Overture.* "I'm comforted by a happy computer," says Tom.

Berry employees, though, must be Tom's biggest secret. At Berry Hardware Company, employees are treated with all the respect of a valued customer. From a typewritten page given to each employee comes this comment:

"We are all members of a very special team pulling together for the same goals. We are very particular about who gets on our team. However, once someone is admitted, they are an honored part of our company and will be treated as such."

Not surprisingly, Tom estimates that three-fourths of his customers are known by name, and "if I don't know their name, they think I know their name."

Everyone is trained to say "yes." That's the magic word at Berry Hardware Company. "What a customer wants to hear is 'yes.' We give 'em 'yes' even if we're not sure. We have a tremendous phone bill from tracking down special items. If we don't have it, we'll get it. Our manager didn't really become effective until he decided I meant it when I said, 'Don't worry about the profit. Worry about the customer.' "

Different, low-budget, and personal. Is Tom Guyton worried that the big chains will steal his secrets? Not at all. "They can't do what I do 'cause Papa doesn't own the store!"

PEN FOODS

*We are going to do a lot of things. But we're not reinventing
the wheel, [and] if it makes sense to us, it will eventually
make sense to our competition.*

—*Norm Pentecost*

You can easily imagine Norm Pentecost as a friendly neighborhood
grocer smiling forever in a Norman Rockwell painting. But while
Pentecost is indeed the kind of guy who will go out of his way to
turn customers into friends, it would be a gross underestimation to
miss the fact that he is also a shrewd businessperson.

Pentecost built his Pen Foods Grocery Store with the customer in
mind. Offering the customer an alternative to chain supermarkets
was the guiding principle from the beginning. Operating out of a
store that was less than half the size of nearby competitors and
starting with no brand identity, Pentecost understood that in order
to succeed his Pen Foods Store would have to be different and serve
customers on a more personal level than found elsewhere.

Pen Foods is a study in ideas. Some new. Most borrowed. And all
but a few offering only a fleeting competitive advantage as Pen
Foods targets an upscale consumer.

"We are going to do a lot of things. But we're not reinventing the
wheel, [and] if it makes sense to us, it will eventually make sense to
to our competition."

Pen Foods is different from the outside in. It is smaller, more
human-sized, a feeling accomplished by design that incorporates
brick arches and multileveled ceilings to give individual departments
a boutique-like atmosphere.

The store is loaded with ideas. Cookbooks are available if you
need to review a favorite recipe so you don't forget important ingredients while you shop. Directional signs are at eye level, making
it easy to locate items on your list. Controlled lighting makes you feel
as though you are shopping in your own pantry. Sharply uniformed
clerks give the appearance that you are surrounded by "your staff."

While little ideas and attention to detail make Pen Foods a pleasant place to shop, the real points of difference are variety and quality. This is where Pentecost stands head and shoulders over his competition. Still, operating out of much smaller quarters is a disadvantage of sorts and requires a constant infusion of even newer ideas.

"Any advantage tended to disappear over time as they [the competition] recognized the value of catering to our upscale customers."

Daring to be different is not without risk. Sometimes it's expensive. The service meat department is a perfect example. Noticing that only one other grocer offered prime beef and fresh veal, Pentecost felt certain there was an untapped market. He asked customers and discovered that indeed there was a demand, and decided to gamble on the purchase of the expensive service cases he would need.

This was a big move for someone who started in business asking, "What kind of mistakes could I make when I don't have deep pockets?" But it proved to be a wise decision. Pen Foods customers will tell you, "If you can't find it at Pen Foods, it just isn't to be found."

That's close to the fact. But the whole truth is that if you can't find it, even at Pen Foods, Norm Pentecost will move mountains to see that it is found. Variety is perhaps the biggest reason why Pen Foods draws customers from as far as sixty miles, at least on an occasional basis.

"In the deli," says Norm, "I want a larger variety of cheeses. And I want to watch faces for puzzled looks. If a customer looks confused, I want our people to go out and help them find what they want. We've probably got it. If we don't have it, I want to get their name and phone number so we can call them when their item comes in. Even if we can't get what they want, I still want that customer called. Calling to say we tried but failed is still delivering on the promise."

Variety, according to Pentecost, is meaningless without quality. Pen's sells one brand of bologna at nearly $5 per pound. Norm agrees that $5 is pretty steep, "unless you like good bologna."

"Products that cost more can demand a higher price, but only if they are worth every penny of it." Pentecost discovered a new brand of bologna on sale in his deli for $1.79 and hit the roof—not because of the low price but because he was certain that the quality would be just as low. He promptly made the deli manager taste, then remove, the offending product. "You'll turn off customers who expect quality and get something else. They won't remember what they paid, only where they bought it."

This brand of thinking explains Pentecost's reaction to a return slip signed by a cashier who refunded a customer $12 for a roast that was too fatty. A closer look revealed that the cashier had indeed gone above and beyond, because the roast had been purchased at a competing store. But Pentecost was upset only because the cashier had failed to offer a substitute at no charge. "It would have cost us $10, but for that $10 we would have had a friend for life."

Variety and quality are the watchwords at Pen Foods. The service meat department regularly offers new surprises to delight the customer. One day it may be stuffed pork chops, the next stuffed chicken, followed by any number of other specialty items.

In the deli, the limit is only your imagination. Pentecost discovered an employee's flair for Mexican-style salsa and ordered labels for "Paula's Own Salsa." One afternoon, he poked his newest goody at us, hot peppers stuffed with cheese and prosciutto ham.

In the wine department, you can choose from "ordinary" to "Rothschild." The same quest for variety as well as the new and different is found in every department.

If variety and quality make Pen Foods different, it is Norm Pentecost himself who makes Pen Foods personal. Norm's marketing is a comfortable, folksy appeal often conducted on radio by Norm himself. Customers don't have to see Norm to feel as though they know Norm, who has carefully crafted his commercials to leave the impression that at Pen Foods "you're dealing with the owner."

"But, believe it or not, I'm very poor with names," says Norm almost apologetically. What he is good at is hiring people who do remember names. Sammi, one of Norm's long-term cashiers, "probably knows 500 to 1,000 names," and even though Norm doesn't do well remembering names, he says, "I like to be friendly."

Pentecost recalls his experience at two nationally known retailers to keep his own service in perspective. "At one, if I can't find what

I'm looking for, they are usually very abrupt with me. At the other, I don't have that problem because I can never find anyone!"

Variety and quality have been Pen Foods's points of difference, while limited resources and a naturally friendly disposition have forced marketing to be low-budget and personal.

A mind that is never too occupied or too proud to spot an idea worth borrowing keeps Pen Foods looking fresh. The whole store is unexpected, involving, and more than a bit out of proportion. It is an elegant example of everyday service that is positively outrageous.

The surprise is that Pen Foods is the work of a man who is basically out of his element. When he opened Pen Foods, Pentecost had little experience in retailing. But he did know people, he understood quality, and he had a personality that became intrinsically intertwined with the name on the door. Norm himself probably best explains his success: "I didn't know retail, but I knew the kind of store I'd be proud to front."

4

TOP O' THE MIND TO YOU!

Mission Statement: *Have fun and try to make the world a better place.*

—*Our Time Associates*

That mission statement is unusual for a "serious" business but it's just perfect for a business that is *not* serious. Business and fun are not mutually exclusive. In fact, one of the best ways to attract attention and build sales is through fun.

It's forty degrees—darn! Too warm to make snow, according to Paul Augustine, snow maker extraordinaire of Hastings, Minnesota. "It's twenty-three degrees below here," he said, sounding far away and just a bit envious of our sunny and relatively warm Texas hill country weather.

"How are you going to use your snow?" he asked, still not sure why an unknown restaurateur would be calling.

"Fun," I told him. "We're going to crank up the compressor and blast out as much snow as possible. Then we're going to throw it, roll in it, or whatever comes to mind."

"Did you say you're in the restaurant business?" He just wanted to make sure. Apparently he doesn't get many phone calls from restaurateurs.

The day before we had decided that there's no business like snow business. Buster (that's right, Buster!) Baldwin, the county commissioner, stopped in for the second or third time that week.

"What are you going to do with that compressor?" he asked while unnecessarily looking at the menu.

"Make snow, if we can figure how it works."

"Oh."

"Oh" is a pretty ordinary response from the guy who placed second in a World Champion Celebrity No-Holds-Barred Charity Crow-off *and* was a guest dipper in the Great Lipton Dip.

Buster, who without much prompting will give you and anyone within about 150 yards a reprise of the crow that earned him second place, noticed an obviously puzzled customer and said, "The food here is excellent, but there isn't another place in town that's this much fun. I come in here pretty often just to make sure I don't miss anything."

Promotions do not have to be borderline bizarre to be effective. Still, since more and more customers are looking for an "experience," or you could say a "relationship," fun is a sure way to win friends and earn top-of-mind positioning. In their book *Positioning: The Battle for Your Mind,* Jack Trout and Al Ries describe positioning as your place in the customer's mind.

You want your company name to be synonymous with the product or service you offer. When a customer needs such a product or service, you want them to think of you first. It's not important for the customer to be able to name all of your competitors, as long as it's your company name that comes up first. This is called being "top of mind." No matter what your business, you want to be top of mind with your customers.

Busy people don't have the time or interest to make complex buying decisions. That means that often business goes not to those who have the best product, service, or price. Instead it goes to the business that wins top-of-mind positioning with the customer. However, this isn't an excuse to concentrate on marketing at the expense of operations.

Top-of-mind positioning can also have the effect of driving customers away, if, immediately upon thinking about the product or service, the customer thinks of you and that thought is immediately followed by the memory of a bad experience.

Remember, please, that the definition of Positively Outrageous Service—

- Random and unexpected
- Out of proportion to the circumstance
- Invites the customer to play or be otherwise highly involved
- Creates compelling word of mouth
- Creates lifetime buying decisions

—is also the definition of the worst service possible. Highly memorable is the hallmark of Positively Outrageous Service, and that, my friends, is positioning.

In the land of the blind, the one-eyed man is king. In other words, it isn't as important to be outstanding as it is to stand out. Many corporate staffing decisions verify this theory. When confronted with the need to fill a vacancy, executives look at the pool of available talent; instead of finding a superior candidate, they often are forced to hire the candidate who is merely the least offensive.

In the best of all worlds you want to be outstanding and you want to stand out. But you also want your competition to be at least pretty good. Otherwise you could end up being painted with the same broad brush as the others.

Fun is a great way to earn top-of-mind positioning. That's not to say that you shouldn't be absolutely fanatical about product and service quality. Just remember to have fun while you are at it!

PRINCIPLES OF PROMOTION

- Be creative.
- Self-promote.
- Involve the community.
- Focus on product quality, not price.

Anyone can give away product. It takes brains to sell it!
—Unknown

Be Creative

Commercials and coupons. It seems that 99.9 percent of marketing people can't think beyond those two budget-busting, tired ideas. Worse, it seems that instead of thinking of really creative ways to attract attention, the trend is to go for large production budgets and deeper discounts. Remember, anyone can give away product. It takes brains to sell it.

Recently a major corporation announced to its operating staff that due to marketing intelligence (an oxymoron), "we have discovered that our major competitor will soon announce an ad campaign that features deep discounts. To preempt this action, we are revising our marketing plan to include an all-new promotion with even deeper discounts."

TWO CORPORATE KIDS
Kid One: I'm gonna discount and you'll be sorry!
Kid Two: Oh yeah? Well, I'll deep discount and you'll really be sorry!
Kid One: Oh yeah? Well, then I'll really, really discount and we'll see who is sorry.
Kid Two: That settles it. I'll give mine away. So put that in your ad budget and smoke it!

Okay, let's see a show of hands. How many of you pay retail for pizzas? Amazing! There are only two hands up. You, sir, may go to the restroom without permission. And you, the guy with the fake nose and glasses . . . oh, you were just kidding? Thank you.

Discount—and it won't be long before the customer figures out what your product is really worth!

If you must discount, do this:

- Give something free with the full-price purchase of some regularly offered item. Do not interpret this to include "buy one, get one's" or other similarly stupid ideas.
- Give a discount for purchases of a package of compatible items. For example, a complete start-up personal computer system might be priced lower than the individual items.

Do not:

- Offer a discount for reduced service, buying during off hours, and so on. Customers will quickly focus on the discounted price as the "true value" of your product.
- Offer a discount on a temporarily stocked item that is not of your usual high quality. Build a reputation for quality and stick to it. Why train customers to believe that less-than-optimum quality is acceptable to you or to them?
- Offer discounts or hold sales on a predictable basis. Do this and you risk training your customers to wait for the sale.

Now that you have a catalog of what not to do, where do you go for ideas that work? Easy! Open your eyes and ears and creative ideas will find you. Here are some places to start looking:

Customers
Employees
Vendors
Industry association
Other businesses (related or not)

Customers are a dynamite source of creative ideas, if you ask. Do you have a lot of customers who are interested in sports? If the answer is yes, why not a sports-related promotion? You get the idea. Find out what turns on your customers and design a promotion that ties in your business with their interests.

We discovered that a lot of our customers were in the business of

65

providing emergency services and created a Firemen's Olympics promotion that will involve many of our customers. The presence of a dozen fire trucks on our property will draw hundreds if not thousands of curious onlookers.

Your employees are another source of creative promotional ideas. Chances are those ideas may need to be modified to suit your budget and to match the promotional strategies that we'll discuss later. Initially, it's likely that your employees will be a bit reluctant to propose anything that's truly outrageous, but give them time. Once they discover that borderline bizarre ideas are encouraged and acted upon, you'll be surprised at how much creativity you've been wasting.

A surprise side effect may very well be an increased sense of creativity in other areas of the job.

Given ownership of creative promotional ideas, employees will work hard to pull them off. They'll soon adopt more playful behavior with your everyday customers, which will further enhance your company's image as a fun, friendly place to do business.

Your vendors are, or at least should be, a source of promotional ideas that work. After all, they service many other companies that are in the same or at least a similar business as you. They are in and out of dozens of businesses every day. Truly heads-up suppliers make it their business to be concerned about your success. And they will be thrilled that you asked for assistance.

Pepsi-Cola Company is one example of what some refer to as a partner in profit. They provide their customers with a "menu" of services available above and beyond their usual excellent delivery of quality canned and bottled drinks and fountain beverage syrups.

Pepsi believes that if they can provide their corporate customers with assistance in such areas as marketing, customer service, management development, and employee retention, then Pepsi can benefit in two ways. First, the customer begins to think of Pepsi as more than a big red, white, and blue truck. Pepsi has earned the position of a true partner. Second, much of the assistance Pepsi provides will eventually translate into greater sales of Pepsi and Pepsi products. Everyone wins.

Look at your own list of vendors. Who is offering help that you haven't accepted? Who could help you if asked? If a vendor isn't knocking on your door to offer assistance, then you should either knock on his door or look for a vendor who is truly interested in your success.

If you are not a member of your industry association—no, make that *active participant* in your industry association—then shame on you! Certainly, many associations are not truly serving the needs of their members. But that is not cause for abandonment. Get in there, pay your dues, and earn the right to do more than raise a little hell. Shake 'em up!

Even if you are the industry leader, participate and participate big. You want all your competition to at least be "pretty good," and the association is there to try to raise the standards. Besides, all the truly great ideas don't come from the big guy.

Associations create the benefit of being able to share ideas with your peers and to learn from experts brought in from the outside. Your association should be a veritable fountain of ideas for promotions.

Perhaps the best sources of ideas will be found outside your industry. Granted, it's not likely that you will find ideas that you can steal intact. But you will find ideas if you are willing to be observant.

Sometimes when you have a particular problem or a specific need for a promotion, the best thing to do is to look at some totally unrelated industry and ask, "How would they do it?" You might be surprised at how, with very little adjustment, you can create an exciting promotion.

Not all that exciting, but a darned good example would be the airlines' frequent-flyer programs. It wasn't long before every airline worth its wings followed suit. Using just a stretch of the imagination, the hotels and car rental agencies also developed frequent-purchaser plans. But how's this for a twist? We considered that if the airlines could have a frequent-flyer program, we could offer a frequent-*fryer* program in our chicken specialty restaurant!

Self-promote

No one has a direct interest in promoting your business other than you. That means if you want public recognition, and you do, then *you* are going to have to let the media know. Sometimes it may mean purchasing air time or ad space. But most of the time if you are doing something really different your coverage will be free. Get to know the local news personalities, and don't hesitate to let them know when you have something of general interest. They want and need news items.

Our snow-making venture is a good example. Once we finally had enough snow on our lot to frame a picture, we had two newspapers out looking for a story. The snow photos didn't make the front page, but when it comes to promotions any mention in the media contributes to the cumulative impression (position) of your operation.

If you make it a habit to call only when you have something that is truly newsworthy, you'll find receptive ears. But you may have to help.

First, give your news people plenty of notice. Don't call an hour before your promotion gets under way and expect a camera crew. When you do contact the media, ask when their schedule is lightest, and try to target your event for a slow news day and a relatively quiet time.

Second, be prepared to help. We write news releases, sometimes entire stories. If you are going to be interviewed, why not write the story beforehand so you can give it to the reporter as he or she leaves? At worst, your material will help prevent errors of fact. At best, it's likely that your story will be published with few or no changes. Why not? It's easier for a reporter to edit written copy than to decipher scribbled notes and start from scratch.

If you are clever, you can get others to promote for you. In its common terms, this is nothing more than word of mouth. It's just that sometimes you need to provide a gentle nudge.

Do something truly different and people will talk anyway. After all, that's the very essence of Positively Outrageous Service. But for the closer-to-ordinary, you must plant the thought.

For example, when I list speaking fees, it is always like this:

- $x speaker's fee.
- Reasonable travel and expenses.
- Upon performance as promised, meeting planner agrees to personally contact two parties who may be interested in my services and make a recommendation.

Just a gentle nudge.

Or take, for example, the letter received by Macaroni's patrons on the night that all meals and drinks are complimentary (see chapter 1). It concludes with the reminder "If you enjoyed your evening at Macaroni's, please tell your friends." Phil Romano could have been much more explicit, but to do so would have been unnecessary, perhaps even tacky. Even counterproductive.

The customer is intuitively aware that generating positive word of mouth is the reasoning behind Romano's largess, and, as long as Romano isn't too overt, the customer is more than willing to play along. But plant the thought he did. And by refusing to spoil the surprise of being treated to a free dinner by overtly soliciting the customer as agent, Romano wins and wins big.

Want to be noticed? Try saying "thank you" in public. A letter to someone's boss or a letter to the editor or to a company newsletter is a great way to say thank you. It's also a great way to be noticed.

Did you chair the local United Way campaign drive? Be certain to write a letter to the editor of your local paper thanking all those who helped.

Want proof that saying thanks is also good marketing? Just as the rough draft of this chapter inched its way out of the printer, our local newspaper arrived. In the letters to the editor, in response to a lengthy thank-you letter I had written a few days earlier, was this wonderful note:

"The gracious letter of Mr. T. Scott Gross thanking others for their contributions in the Toys for Tots effort is no doubt characteristic of this young man. His leadership and compassion stirred this community to action in this special Christmas appeal. The very generous and caring community has Mr. Gross to thank for his 'quarterbacking' this one."

How do you feel so far? Self-serving? Sneaky? You do? Good!

Still, the truth is this: Doing what is right and good for the customer is the best thing to do. If you do it because you love others, that's fine. You'll receive the recognition you deserve. If you do good things solely for the recognition, fine. At least you did something good that made a difference.

Good guy or bad guy, doing good things comes back to your business. So whether you are a saint or a snake, looking out for others is definitely what you want to do.

It's an old saw that you cannot help others unless you first take care of yourself. It doesn't matter where you are or what you are doing. Act like a good guy and make certain to make your identity synonymous with your business. If you are the owner/operator of Acme Hardware, you want to be known as Mr. Hardware. Whatever business you own or manage, it's your job to create a strong positive identity with your company name and product and all the good works you and your business do, for whatever motivation.

You are serving outrageously when you have so established your position that whenever the product you sell or the service you provide is mentioned, the only name that comes to mind is either yours or your company's. Say one and automatically think the other. That's solid positioning, and Positively Outrageous Service is how it is done.

Involve the Community

We sat with a group of franchisees at a meeting called to discuss marketing strategy. One deep, deep discount promotion after another was unveiled by the representative from corporate marketing. Unable or unwilling to hold my tongue, I finally stood and said, "There are two sayings that come to mind. First, anyone can give away product. It takes brains to sell it. And, second, a sale without a profit is a donation.

"Of course, the company gets its royalty payments right off the top, so perhaps their concern is limited to short-term cash flow rather than the long-term health of our business.

"If the best promotion you can think of is nothing more than a deep discount, here's a way to save a lot of money: Eliminate the marketing department and let the accounting department declare a hefty discount on the product of their choice!"

I thought I was making progress when a fellow, and obviously frightened, franchisee said, "Nice thoughts. But I have competition within several blocks of me in either direction, and I have to discount."

I tried again, this time dragging out my pizza analogy.

"Could I see a show of hands of how many people pay full retail for pizza?"

There were none.

"Okay, so why do you want to participate in training your customers to think that the true value of your product is the discounted price?"

Glazed eyes. I quit.

I had visions of other meetings somewhere in our town where other frightened franchisees of our competition's chains were meeting. And in every meeting someone was saying, "I have competition within several blocks of me in either direction, and I have to discount."

And no one considered creative ways to sell product—only "last gasp" ideas about how to give it away.

Face it, discounting works—but only short term and only to build traffic. Do it regularly and you'll train your customers to wait for the sale.

Now the catch is there are some customers who *only* buy "on-deal." I call these people "on-dealers." They won't set foot in your business for any reason other than a sale. Turn your sales into money losers and all you've done is generate the traffic of on-dealers plus encouraged your regular customers to trade from a purchase with RPM (reasonable profit margin) to a purchase with very low profit, if any.

Do this often enough and you risk turning your good RPM customers into "Pizzas"—people who would be regular customers if you hadn't trained them to wait for the sale.

Retailers may not have created on-dealers, but they are certainly guilty of encouraging them. Worse, they've created a special discount called the "anyway discount."

Earlier we said that the definition of Positively Outrageous Service works for both the best and the worst service you've ever experienced. In several ways the same can be said for the definition of outrageous promotion. A surprise freebie can go a long way in creating customer interest and loyalty. But such a freebie in the form of an anyway discount is a sure way to guarantee lower profits.

Many retailers create elaborate promotional materials and ad campaigns designed to drive consumers into their stores. We've already commented on the value of creating traffic among the on-dealers. But there will be those potential full-price (RPM) customers who truly do need a little incentive to give you a try.

Marketers call this "creating trial." The theory is that by giving a new customer a special incentive to try your product or service, you so enchant them that they will become regulars.

That's the theory.

In reality, there are only so many potential new customers in your market. So repeatedly hitting the market with promotional discounts, especially on regular products or service, only works to turn good, paying, RPM customers into Pizzas ("We'll wait for the sale").

Still, assuming that a promotional campaign that features discounts does make sense, marketers totally destroy the point by offering "anyway discounts." This they accomplish by plastering every available square inch of wall (even air) space with posters touting the discounted deal.

Why?

The customers who came in because they saw the commercial or read the ad already know about the deal. Discounting to these on-dealers is bad enough. Why tell your RPM customers that they too should trade down to a lower-profit-margin sale? They were coming in *anyway!*

Case in point: My wife and I are very fond of a chicken sandwich offered by one of our clients. It sells for about $3 and is worth every penny of the price. It is top quality and absolutely delicious.

Returning from a trip, we left the airport for the long drive home. Hungry and in a hurry, we decided that the mile or so detour to this particular chain restaurant would be made up by their fast drive-through service. Besides, we wanted quality food and were willing to pay in both time and dollars.

When we pulled onto the lot, there on the marquee was a notice advising, "Any two sandwiches on the menu—$2.99." I'm sorry, but this is outrageously poor marketing. I was willing to pay $6 for our two sandwiches. The quality, flavor, and service made them a value. But, no! Some unthinking marketing mogul said, "Let's give them a discount . . . *anyway!"*

Discounting is a short-term cover-up of long-term problems. If you must discount to survive, your prices are too high, your service is too poor, or your quality is too low. There is a better way.

What do you do? You establish a personal relationship with your community of customers. You give them another, better, more profitable reason to patronize your business. We'll look at specific strategies for "wowing the customer" later in this chapter.

Focus on Product Quality, Not Price

It's okay to remember that product and service are in many ways synonymous. Service is less tangible than most products. But don't underestimate its lingering impact on customers' feelings about your business.

Think about it. Have you ever heard, can you even imagine, compelling word of mouth over low prices? Oh, sure! You do hear stories about some hard-bargaining consumer beating a car salesman to a price-pulp. But those stories are rare and almost always told with a sinister grin rather than a straight-from-the-heart smile.

To paraphrase an old saying, "The effects of quality linger long after the thrill of a cheap price is forgotten."

So here's a novel concept just made for a comeback in the 90's: Focus on quality. In the 90's you won't be able to separate quality products from the quality of the service included with the deal.

Positively Outrageous Service practically demands that promotions focus on product quality, not price.

FOUR GUIDELINES FOR PROMOTIONS

- Have fun.
- Get people to your store.
- Get people involved with your product.
- Do something good for others.

Have Fun

Having fun is a guiding principle of Positively Outrageous Service, and your promotions should be no different. Promotions that have a tongue-in-cheek feel generate far more excitement than a simple discount.

Fun promotions give your business a Feel Good atmosphere that most customers find hard to resist. The danger here is that your customers stop taking you seriously when it comes to product and service. Fun or not, promotions should never be allowed to interfere with product and service.

Occasionally you should mix in a more serious promotion, just to let your customers know that you still have your eye on the ball.

Get People to Your Store

We do not participate in any promotional effort that does not have as its ultimate goal to get people into our store. Period.

Take, for example, the Christmas we got the bright idea to make snow. After dozens of phone calls, we managed to acquire a small snow gun, rent a room-sized compressor, and borrow several hundred feet of fire hose from a local volunteer fire department—all the ingredients you need to make snow except biting cold weather and a full measure of insanity.

(We did manage to make snow. Not a lot, but it was snow. It took four or five miserable attempts, mostly in the wee hours of the morning. I'm adding these remarks just to save you the agony. Considering the effort and expense, it was one of my most stupid ideas.)

Several people suggested that it would be easier to move our equipment to a nearby park and draft icy river water into our snow-making apparatus. True, but it would have meant locating the stunt away from the store. And, to our way of thinking, it would have made our efforts pointless.

There are hundreds of charity events in which your business could participate, and you can't be involved in everything. So why not save your resources for events that bring people to your property?

Every year in our town there is a charity basketball tournament. And every year we are called on to purchase advertising in the program. Every year we say "no," knowing full well that the participants are 95 percent out-of-towners and such expenditures would be a complete waste.

Spend money but avoid flat-out donations whenever possible. Apply financial muscle when both you *and* others will benefit.

When we are approached with a request that would in no way enhance either our immediate sales or our standing in the community, we politely decline and then suggest how we would be willing to participate.

In the case of the basketball tournament, we give several hundred free-drink cards, one for each participant. Most of these are redeemed, and the majority lead to a purchase of lunch or dinner. So we win, they win, and no bucks get flushed into worthless program ads.

Get People Involved with Your Product

Great salespeople know that selling is most often nothing more than matching a customer need with a product solution. Once the customer gets the product into her hands, if it meets her needs for quality and price, then the sale is a done deal. It follows then that promotions that put your product in your customers' hands will result in sales.

Most of your promotional events should in some way involve your customers with your product.

Giving out small trial samples is the purest form of promotion. It's one of the most overlooked, and it's also one of the least expensive.

Every year we serve as the starting point for the March of Dimes Walk. The walk both begins and ends at our restaurant. As the walkers arrive at the finish line—our dining room—they are greeted with a small sample of soft drink and a piece of hot, delicious fried chicken.

Our cost is about thirty-five cents per trial. Cheap! Compare that with direct mail, television, or any other form of marketing, and you'll see that in terms of getting our product into the mouth of a potential customer, sponsoring this event is the best promotional deal in town.

Of course, many of the walkers are regular customers. For them, it's a simple thank you for participating in a worthy cause. Besides, we make plenty of money on their regular patronage, so what's a free piece of chicken now and then?

Another example of getting customers involved with our product is the annual Taste of the Town, sponsored by our local restaurant association. We get right in there with the fancy hotels and fine-dining operations. We drive our gleaming, oven-equipped delivery van right onto the exhibition floor and are proud as peacocks to serve a dynamite product from the back of our van.

Who cares if the booths on either side are staffed with European chefs? We usually make quite a splash, and people are amazed at how well our product compares with the rest.

What amazes me is that every year during the organizational meetings, some restaurateur pipes up and says, "We should limit the number of tickets. Otherwise we might have to give away too much food."

Of course, dummy! That's the point! Getting the customer involved with your product increases sales, provided your product is good. Sampling is the least expensive way in the world to get trial.

The secret to sampling is to make certain that your samples are large enough to tease but too small to satisfy.

Timing is also important in effective sampling. For example, assuming that the average participant in the March of Dimes Walk takes two hours to complete the walk, would you want to start the march at 8:00 A.M. or 10:00 A.M.? Remember, the finish line is a restaurant!

If you are really creative, the product can be the promotion. You'll see a great example in just a bit when we tell you about the Great Lipton Dip.

Do Something Good for Others

The best promotions do something good for others. People are much more inclined to turn out for a good cause than for the simple lining of your pocket. This is also true of the media. In fact, a major principle for marketing on a budget is to do as much promotion as possible that involves charity projects.

When you are doing a good deed for others, it is much easier to get free publicity. The charity organization itself often has an effective communications network that can guarantee a large turnout. Be discreet enough not to turn every event into a blatant sales pitch and your promotions will position both you and your product as the quality choice.

What you must do to ensure that your promotions work for both you and the charity is to spend time showing people how to get you to say yes.

Often we are approached by community organizations with proposals that, to their way of thinking, we should be both complimented and thrilled to accept. Most people have no idea about the thin margins of profit that keep most businesses afloat. They see traffic at your store and assume that you are laughing all the way to the bank. For most businesses, by the time the checks are written to cover rent, payroll, and product costs, that laugh is not much more than a quiet chuckle or maybe only a sigh of relief.

We were recently offered the concession rights to a local charity event in exchange for a "token donation of $2,000." Asked how we were selected for this dubious honor, we were told, "Because you do so many good things for the community, we wanted you to have a chance to make something, too."

Unfortunately, when we looked at the projected size of the crowd, it would have been to our benefit to donate $250 and beg them to invite one of our competitors to handle it!

People just don't understand your business.

Don't say no. Teach them how to get you to a yes.

We start by giving our rules for promotion:

> Have fun.
> Get people to the store.
> Get people involved with your product.
> Do something good for others.

We also explain that, because our resources are limited, the best way to get us involved is to ask well in advance so that they can be included in our budget. It's amazing the number of people who want you to donate to an event that is planned for tomorrow.

Perhaps the number-one request we get is for a cash donation. "Never" is a pretty big word, so whatever is the closest word to "never" is how often you should give cash. Give product—product for the group to use or auction—but try to always give product. Your product is your business, and at the very least a donation should expose more people to your product.

It may be possible that some charity or community interest events can't use your product, but I can't think of any. In that event, donate time instead, and avoid cash donations whenever possible. I'm not talking about the $10 here and there to buy raffle tickets for the local church or cookies for the scouts. I'm talking about the $50, $100, and $1,000 amounts that would do you as much good as smoking it.

If you are absolutely Hell-bent on giving cash, occasionally give a customer a 100 percent discount. You'll start more tongues wagging than you could with a dozen cash donations.

The Great Lipton Dip

We noticed that a restaurant chain that offered quart-sized insulated travel mugs of tea with refills at a low price had struck gold with the idea. Customer after customer zoomed through their drive-through, handing in their mugs for refills and almost always ordering lunch or dinner.

We looked into a similar program for our single-unit operation and soon found that it was cost-prohibitive. We could find cheap mugs at a reasonable price, but we were committed to either offering a quality product or dropping the project. We wanted a mug that was so nice people would want to keep it in their vehicle.

Not willing to compromise, we contacted Aladdin Synergetics, makers of the mug, and attempted to negotiate a lower price, hoping that by going direct we could get the price into our range. The good people at Aladdin agreed that, because we were a franchise of a large chain and a success for us would turn into a success for them, they would give us a special price.

That's the good news.

The bad news is that our tea-mug brainstorm didn't hit us until the first week in October, nearly the end of the iced-tea season. Besides, we had a mondo-bizarro idea for introducing the mug: the Great Lipton Dip.

We had seen the Nestea Plunge commercials and thought if Nestea can plunge then perhaps Lipton could dip.

The folks at Lipton saw the possibilities and agreed to help us. Rather than putting them on the hook, let's just say they were extremely generous.

The plan: At 5:15 on Halloween local celebrities would do the Lipton Dip into a twelve-foot swimming pool of iced Lipton Tea. Each celebrity would be given a bag containing $100 in nickels to pour into the pool. Twenty thousand nickels later, eighteen girls, six each from the three local high schools, would be invited to go "diving for dollars" in the great "splash for cash." The only rule: All money must go over the side of the pool in one of our new tea mugs.

Even our neighboring K Mart got into the act, by supplying the

79

pool. J. C. Penney helped us with the nickels.

We were allowed to do the morning show on a local radio station, got remote coverage from two radio stations, and found ourselves on the front page of the local papers two days in a row.

Total cost to us: less than $100.

By the way, the girls, representing their high school cheerleading, dance, and drill teams, were able to recover $993.70 in ten minutes.

The Great Lipton Dip:

> Was fun;
> Got hundreds of people to the store;
> Got people involved with (in!) the product; and
> Did something good for others.

In true outrageous fashion, the promo was unexpected and out of proportion, invited the customers to play, created compelling word of mouth, and, through the idea of refillable, forever tea mugs, created lifetime buying decisions!

COROLLARIES

- Get someone else to pay for your promo.
- Reward everyone, if possible.
- Allow for vicarious participation.
- Don't always try to make money.
- Have specific, measurable goals.

Get Someone Else to Pay for Your Promo

Look around. You may be surprised at how many partners you have with a major interest in your success. True partners share both the profits and the risks. But there are others who also have a vested interest in your sales. These are the ones to tap for help with promotions.

Every year millions of dollars in marketing funds go unspent. This is an even greater tragedy than the zillions that are spent foolishly. Almost every major manufacturer has a co-op marketing fund. This is money that is specifically set aside to assist their customers in marketing. Ask for your share! And, while you're at it, ask for your competitor's share. He probably won't use it, so you should!

If you are part of a chain and you are doing something creative, it's fair to imply that your success could lead to greater sales chain-wide. This even works on nonapproved suppliers. Ask for their help with the promise that if the product is successful at your location, it has a much greater chance of being approved for chain-wide use. You'll be surprised at how much muscle can be put against a local effort.

One surprise source of promotion dollars is other businesses in the neighborhood. If you have an event up your sleeve that is going to draw hundreds, perhaps thousands, of people to your location, neighboring businesses will also benefit. Ask and chances are they will help pay. One of our best such events was the Great Ping-Pong Promo.

We decided to drop 3,000 Ping-Pong balls on our parking lot, each good for a prize. We went to neighboring businesses and literally sold ad space on Ping-Pong balls. Each ball was numbered. Customers who retrieved a ball had to take it to the center court of a nearby mall and consult a board posted there to find out what prize they had won.

They took their ball to the appropriate merchant to retrieve their prize. But, in addition to the merchant-supplied prize, each winner was given a card good for a free drink at our restaurant. That created incredible traffic for us and marked the beginning of a series of similarly bizarre promotions, as well as a string of incredible sales increases. Our share of the expense was less than $250!

The promotion was such a hit that local merchants began calling to see what was coming next and ask if they could participate. Anytime you can get 3,000-plus people to your property for less than $250, you've got a winning idea.

Reward Everyone, If Possible

Promotions that offer only a few opportunities to win often end up disappointing many who perceive themselves as losers. The best promotions are those in which everyone is a winner.

Several years ago, we were approached by the school district to provide rewards for students who qualified for the honor roll. That's an admirable thing to do, but what about the thousands of kids who are trying but for one reason or another haven't managed to make the grade?

We like to treat all our guests as winners and wondered how we could reward more kids without killing ourselves on cost. We decided to create a Pays for A's program in which each student would receive a business card–sized coupon good for one to ten free drinks. The teachers circle one free drink for each A on the report card.

True, some bright youngsters come in and proudly order up a half dozen or more free drinks for themselves and friends or family. (It's also good to see the smile on the face of the kid who only qualified for a single free drink. That may have been his first A ever. Hopefully, because it was possible for everyone to come out a winner, it won't be his last!)

Allow for Vicarious Participation

Bill Behling, director of dining services for PFM, the food-service provider at Beloit College, is a master of the borderline bizarre. He also has a keen understanding of human nature.

Bill says that while everyone likes to have a good time, not everyone wants to participate personally. They want to participate vicariously, in what Bill calls nonparticipative participation. Besides, Bill's budget won't allow him to do something truly spectacular for all of his student diners.

His solution: Spotlight Specials.

Bill has constructed a stage in the center of the student dining hall, where he serves a selected group of volunteer diners one of his

Spotlight Specials while the remaining students participate in safe anonymity.

One of Bill's best-loved Spotlight Specials is breakfast in bed. The waitstaff outfit themselves in curlers, mudpacks, and scuff slippers in a college student's parody of "Mom" as they serve the pajama-clad students who wait impatiently in their beds. The stage, of course, has been outfitted to resemble a dorm room.

Bill's favorite is the Spotlight Dinner, where tuxedoed waitpersons serve a gourmet steak and lobster dinner to formally attired student diners at candle-lit tables on center stage.

Bill believes that Positively Outrageous Service is especially important in his operation because he has a trapped audience. Rather than let boredom set in and risk losing customers when it's time to renew meal tickets, Bill keeps 'em guessing with random and unexpected nonpromotion promotion.

Another Beloit favorite is the Blazing Saddle Special, in which the meal offering consists entirely of bean dishes. Students and staff are invited to dress as though they were in the movie *Blazing Saddles.* Bill says the students are crazy over this one. Even though such a promotion must be great for food cost, I think I'll pass on this one. Come to think about it, I guess everyone will!

Don't Always Try to Make Money

Occasionally you need to run a promotion "just because." Maybe it's to say thanks to your customers. Maybe it's just to say thanks.

Our favorite "just because" promotion is called the Wing and a Prayer Celebration. In-house we call it our Belly and Soul Promo. In a few words, we go in on Christmas Day and, with the help of volunteer employees and customers, cook up hundreds of dinners. We give these dinners to local church groups for them to distribute as they see fit.

We tell them, "We'll fill the belly if you will fill the soul. Find hungry people, and feel free to define hunger any way you see fit."

Here's a letter to the editor from the pastor of one of the participating churches.

> Restaurant owners and staff deserve thanks. I would not want an-
> other Christmas season to go by without expressing our special
> thanks to the owners, Scott and Melanie Gross of our city, for their
> annual exhibit of Christian charity and concern for the hungry of our
> community.
>
> How fortunate we are to have people like these as part of our
> community. Thank you!

Try to pay for that kind of publicity. You can't. Besides, there's
plenty of value in doing something nice "just because."

For you hard-nosed businesspeople it should be said that for that
kind of promotion we get thanked every day. Our customers thank
us at the cash register. Occasionally they let us know that their
patronage is due to more than good products and friendly service.

Recently a woman came in and told us she wasn't one of our
customers but was trying us because of our good work in the
community. Her thank you turned out to be the biggest sale of the
day. More good news: She's now a regular.

Have Specific, Measurable Goals

We spent thousands on display advertising and radio before we
discovered that it had been an absolute, total waste of money.

Our worst failure was a display ad featuring a coupon redeemable
for a free order of french fries with any purchase. I calculated that
we spent $141.50 for each order of free french fries given away. What
a colossal waste!

While it's impossible to predict the response you will get on any
promotion, it makes sense to at least begin with an idea of the size
of the response required for the promotion to break even. Before
you proceed, always ask, "Can I think of any more effective or at
least promising way to achieve my marketing goals?"

Since the free french fry fiasco, I have often wondered what kind
of response we would have had if we had taken the same budget,
converted it into crisp $5 bills, and simply dropped them into carry-
out bags at random. We could attach a card that reads, "Thanks for
being our customer. Please use this to treat a friend on your next

visit." I'll bet the word of mouth would have been phenomenal. We'll try that someday . . .

Sometimes the only way you can measure the effectiveness of a marketing strategy is to stop. We stopped and discovered that sales didn't change one iota. That's not to say that radio and newspapers don't work, only that what we were doing wasn't right for us. Today we use both radio and newspapers, but our tactics—and results —have changed.

Several times a year we use coupons. When we do, we measure results carefully. We now have a hit list of our top ten coupon offers. When we coupon, we always lead with three of our top ten offers and experiment with the fourth position on the sheet. It would be easy to just fill all four coupon positions with offers with guaranteed pulling power. The downside is that you would never know if it was time for a new idea. So we lead with three surefire winners and take our best shot on the fourth in hopes of finding another winner.

As with any promotion, we forecast sales without coupons, compare that with sales with coupons, factor in distribution and discount costs, and determine the true value of the promotion. Notice that the only reason we are concerned with the number of coupons redeemed is to determine which coupons work best. Otherwise we don't care how many coupons actually come back. The only thing that matters is the increase in sales. The reason for this is that we usually get a sales response greater than can be accounted for by the number of coupons redeemed.

We think this is because the coupons serve to remind customers who haven't been in in a while that it's time to come and see us again. They know they'll be getting quality products and friendly service, reason enough to shop with us.

WOWING THE CUSTOMER

- Remember the customer even when he is not buying.
- Support causes the customer holds important.
- Give something free of cost and occasion.
- Become a product and service fanatic.

- Entertain the customer (especially while she is waiting).
- Demonstrate that the customer is first by respecting his time.
- Say you are sorry for the slightest slip from standard.
- Ask for the customer's opinion.
- Promote internally.
- Know the customer by name.
- Invite the customer to play.

Remember the Customer Even When He Is Not Buying

Mr. Muldoon, manager of the IGA grocery in Covington, Kentucky, knows his business. And the only way to really know your business is to know your customers.

When grandmotherly Ruby Rekers left town for vacation, she forgot to tell her grocer, which, if you think about it, is no big deal. That is, unless your grocer is Muldoon. As Mrs. Rekers turned the key in her front door upon her return, the phone was ringing off the hook. It was Muldoon, worried because he couldn't locate a valued customer.

Muldoon practices business one customer at a time. This is a good lesson for any business, regardless of size. In this age of computers, there is no excuse for losing track of a customer. Further, every customer should be the personal responsibility of a single employee who is assigned the task of monitoring his or her purchasing habits. Any change should generate a personal phone call, to allow problems to be discovered and corrected as soon as possible.

The mere fact that you notice when a customer has been out for a while has tremendous positive impact. It cements that relationship that says, "This is my place. They know me and care about me as well as my business."

Support Causes
the Customer Holds Important

When we opened our restaurant in a community that was new to us, we asked the banker, contractor, and city officials what charity organization had the widest support of the community. "Hospice" was the most common response. So we took the cue and held a preopening party, as a training exercise, and suggested that attendees donate the menu price of their meal to the hospice.

Neither the community nor the hospice has forgotten.

Robert Love is a regular. On a recent visit we discovered that his grandmother was in the hospital. Grandma loves our food.

"How's Grandma's appetite?" we asked.

"Fine. She gets out tomorrow and wants to stop here on the way home!"

We didn't think Grandma should have to wait. Minutes later Grandma's meal was delivered. On the house, of course.

You can't support every cause. So choose causes that have high visibility among *your* customer base. And when you support a cause, give it more than lip service. Support it with your time, talent, and dollars. Your customers will notice and come to the cash register to thank you personally.

It is surprising what will grab the attention of your customers. Things you do that you think are above and beyond may get little notice. Sometimes things that you do in the normal course of business will turn out to be surprise hits with your customers.

We decided that our dining area wasn't getting the attention it needed. We were getting too busy to love on our customers and keep the area looking its best. When you are too busy to love on the customers, you are too darned busy. Your unloved customers will help you get things back in balance by staying away, so that you'll have fewer customers to worry over.

Our solution was to find a learning-disabled person and train her as a dining room attendant. We looked for the friendliest, most loving individual we could find. We gave little weight to experience and possible ability to perform tasks beyond routine cleaning. In-

told our gal that her main job was to make absolutely
t every customer was made to feel as if they were a guest
ie.

Has it worked? You bet!

Three-quarters of all customer comment cards mention our dining
room attendant by name. Many say that she is the reason we get their
business. And, of course, our regulars are often greeted with more
than a smile—they get a hug.

Support causes that are important to your customers, and be
willing to be surprised at what really turns them on.

Give Something Free of Cost and Occasion

Paul Russell, speaker/consultant from Olathe, Kansas, says that Las
Vegas slot machines are equipped with "discouragement detectors."
He says that a little eye in the machine senses when you are on the
last pull before moving on and keeps your attention by signaling the
machine to dispense a few more coins.

Psychology 101 taught us that intermittent reinforcement is necessary to perpetuate a behavior. This idea of random, unexpected
reinforcement is the basis of Positively Outrageous Service. Occasionally you should do something for your customers that is totally
unexpected. Not only is this a great way to say thank you to the
people who make the payments on your house and car, it is also a
great way to shape behavior.

We have used the principle to build a second lunch run, as
described in chapter 1. The prize: lunch trade from an almost-too-
distant high school. The bait: fresh-baked, hot-from-the-oven white
chocolate macadamia nut cookies.

The students have a limited lunch hour, so fast service is a must.
The good news is that their orders are so predictable we can start
cooking before they arrive. To encourage their regular patronage we
occasionally slip one of our gourmet cookies on their tray.

One evening a young lady came in and ordered two dozen
cookies. "What cookies?" we asked. "We don't have cookies on
the menu."

"Yes you do," she insisted. "I've gotten them here twice at lunch. I told my mom about them, and she said they sounded so good that she sent me to buy two dozen."

We were out of cookies, or we would have asked her to wait while we baked some and then just given them to her.

"I guess my mom will just have to start eating here for lunch."

Good idea.

Become a Product and Service Fanatic

Be a product and service quality fanatic. Nothing tells the customer that she is important like being fanatical over getting the product, service, and order perfect.

In addition to making the customer happy, true quality fanaticism creates legends. That's the compelling word of mouth that marks service that is truly outrageous.

Everyone has heard the story about the Federal Express driver who wrestled the entire drop box into his truck when he couldn't find the key and didn't want the packages to miss the flight.

That story came from one of Tom Peters's books, along with the story of the night janitor at a Domino's Pizza warehouse who braved heavy weather and the potential wrath of his supervisor when he left the job to deliver pizza dough to a unit that otherwise would have run out.

But you need not be intimidated by such stories. Go ahead and settle for the title of "ordinary fanatic"! You don't have to be faster than a speeding bullet or able to leap tall buildings in a single bound. You only have to care.

And caring pays off.

The phone rang as I walked by. I had only stopped to check on the store. If you are an owner or manager, then you have both heard and used that phrase. "Checking on the store" is a great way to turn a two-minute pit-stop into an evening-long marathon.

The customer was calling to complain that we had delivered an order of eight pieces of dark chicken instead of the eight-piece mixed order he had requested.

"Can you send someone with some white meat?"

"I'm Scott Gross, the owner. Our vans are out at the moment, but I have your address right here, and if you don't mind an unmarked vehicle, I'll bring it out right away."

"I don't mind waiting on one of your vans," he offered.

"I do."

When I arrived at the doorstep, he was waiting with one of our bags, containing four pieces of dark meat.

"Thank you, but you can keep that. We can't use it once it has been delivered."

"Well, I just didn't want to beat you out of extra chicken. All I need is four pieces of white meat."

"That's nice of you, but we've replaced your entire order. Chicken, biscuits, potatoes, and cole slaw, and that comes complete with our apologies. Put the original delivery in the refrigerator and save it for tomorrow. If it tastes a little like leftovers tomorrow, I won't feel guilty. But tonight your order should be as hot, fresh, and delicious as possible."

An hour later my home phone rang. It was my mother calling to report an incident at the local grocery store. It seems that, as she was shopping, a lady stopped her with these words: "You won't believe what one of your kids just did."

Expecting the worst, Mom was both relieved and proud to hear that our special delivery customer had taken time to call several of his neighbors to tell them about our fanatical service and to invite them to share the extra food.

Entertain the Customer (Especially While She Is Waiting)

Don't tell me that entertainment just isn't your thing, because if it isn't, it should be.

People don't like to wait. Anything you can do to capture their attention will make the wait seem less painful and the overall experience much more pleasant. Waiting will be a 90's no-no. The best thing to do is to eliminate waits. The best thing is to make them disappear by entertaining the customer.

The masters of wait-line entertainment are the folks at Disney. Next time you are at a Disney park notice that in many instances there are things to do or watch while you are in line. One of my favorites is the line to the Space Ride at Disneyland.

You wander—that's right, wander—through a simulated space-port. The sounds of futuristic preflight announcements and take-offs are complemented by video commercials touting trips to the outer reaches of the solar system. Space craft and characters from the movie *Star Wars* are so enchanting, so entertaining, that the only thing better than the wait is the ride itself.

Not every wait can be, or should be, Disneyesque. But they should all be at the very least pleasant and, when possible, interesting.

Wometco Theatres in Florida is building new cinemas that feature special viewing windows that allow waiting patrons a firsthand look at the inner workings of the projection booth. First-timers are often startled to learn that the booth is not a booth at all but a block-long room running above the auditoria. They are surprised to discover that there are no reels, only giant platters that enable the film to run in one continuous loop, eliminating the need to rewind.

The cost is minimal, and the result is patrons who feel much more a part of the operation.

On a smaller scale, other movie theater chains are offering pre-movie announcements. In a personal touch reminiscent of bygone days, theater managers are addressing their audiences with a personal welcome and interesting facts about the movie and its stars.

As the leisure-starved consumers of the 90's become ever more selective about how they spend their time, and their money, it will be increasingly important to eliminate the wait. And where that is not possible, make it at least appear shorter than it is. Use your imagination. Talk to your employees. Ask your customers. You will discover that there is something you can do that will be far more effective and creative than fresh magazines in the reception area.

Demonstrate That the Customer Is First by Respecting His Time

The phone rings. You answer. A pleasant voice says, "Will you please hold for Mr. Smith?" You think, *"Jerk!"*

If you really want to offend someone, treat them as though their time—and therefore they themselves—is of no value or consequence. How many times have you been left waiting and had this thought: "Do they think I don't have anything better to do with my time than this?"

On the other hand, if you really want to *wow* the customer, treat his time as a precious commodity. If you must make him wait, at least acknowledge his presence immediately. Check back with frequent progress reports, apologize each time, and, as previously mentioned, do something, anything, to make the wait as pleasant and interesting as possible.

What is worse than waiting in a long line? Waiting in a long line when all you need is a question answered or something relatively insignificant.

When we have a customer at the drive-through who needs only a cold drink, rather than cause him to wait even a minute, we run the drink to his car to allow him to shortcut the line and be on his way.

Other customers don't seem to mind. In fact, quickly eliminating very small purchases clears the way for us to get started on the customers who follow. Every business should consider some form of express service targeted directly at customers for whom speed of service is a priority. They will appreciate the consideration and remember you when they need the deluxe treatment. It would be a mistake to assume that express service applies only to retailers. Insurance companies, public utilities, government agencies, and providers of medical care should be listening as well.

Better than making waiting a pleasant science, why not do whatever possible to eliminate waiting?

Better yet, why not learn to operate on the customer's schedule? One of society's institutionalized insanities is the attitude of tele-

phone companies when a new customer orders s/
there on the eleventh between 9:00 A.M. and 5:/

"Like I haven't got anything better to do than t
installer."

Heads-up competitors will listen to their customers,
trends hour by hour, and tailor their services to meet custom
needs.

Most restaurants, theme parks, movie theaters, and even auto
dealers now operate on customer time. There is still room for improvement for hotels, where we must check in and out to suit their
convenience and where we rent rooms by the day even when that
doesn't always meet our needs.

The biggest improvement can and must come from small retailers
and service companies, who too often insist on keeping business
hours instead of customers' hours. Why are they surprised that the
major retailers who remain open evenings and weekends are able to
capture so much of the market? A need to purchase doesn't always
arise on Monday through Friday between nine and five.

If a need itches, fill it!

Say You Are Sorry for the
Slightest Slip from Standard

When our customers must wait more than one minute for their food
to cook, we offer a courtesy drink. This small apology helps make
the wait more pleasant. It also tells the customer that we are serious
about our business and value their time.

> THE POSITIVELY OUTRAGEOUS SERVICE RULES FOR APOLOGY
> · When in doubt—apologize.
> · Apologize even when the customer doesn't know you
>   goofed.
> · Always make amends in excess of the slip-up.
> · Empower everyone to solve problems.
> · Handle mistakes by the numbers.

When in doubt—apologize. The idea of being right has little value to the outrageous server. If the customer perceives a slight or a mistake, then forget about being right. The customer is right.

Take your lumps, apologize, and waste absolutely no time explaining why things happened the way they did.

Apologize.

Make amends.

Explain what you will do to prevent future occurrences.

Apologize again.

Apologize even when the customer doesn't know you goofed. An unexpected apology has such positive and lasting impact that it is almost worth creating situations that you can use. Dropping in an extra biscuit, saying, "You waited just a little too long to suit us, so here's a biscuit to munch on the way home," is such a pleasant surprise. This is especially true when the customer didn't think the wait was very long anyway.

A dry cleaner can pin on a small mending kit and say, "I really wanted to have this for you yesterday." An auto dealer can say, "One of our mechanics leaned against the fender and smudged it a bit, so we had your car washed and waxed to make up for it."

We routinely apologize to customers who wait for more than a second or two in our drive-through. "Sorry to keep you waiting" is a favorite line, especially when we say it just as the customer rolls down the window. Sometimes we'll say, "Hi! I'll be back with you in a New York second." And then only a few seconds later we say, "Thanks for being patient. Are you ready to order?"

And the customer thinks, "If they apologize for service like this, I don't think I could handle what they call really good service."

Mike Bates of the Widman Popcorn Company was enjoying lunch with a friend at a Red Lobster Restaurant. According to Mike, the service was friendly and fast and the food right on target. Imagine his surprise when the manager approached the table and explained that, because it took eleven minutes, rather than the promised ten, the entire meal would be on the house. Now guess who is one of Red Lobster's most loyal customers! And all for the price of lunch!

Always make amends in excess of the slip-up. An apology should be so out of proportion to the offense that the customer feels absolutely overwhelmed.

Not long ago I was introduced to a fellow customer at our local computer store. I told him that he looked familiar. "I think you were at our place for lunch today." He said that it had been the day before and that he really enjoyed the restaurant. When I asked him why, his answer made me uncomfortable at first. Having had time to think about it, it was quite a compliment.

"We get lunch for the office pretty regularly, and over the years on two occasions our order was completely confused. It's possible that it was our fault, but the result is the same—a messed-up order."

"And that's why you like us?" I was beginning to think this guy was kinky!

"Of course not. It's just that when it has happened, you people have gone absolutely overboard to set things right. No one likes to order one thing and get something else. But isn't it nice to know that if it isn't just perfect, someone will make a major production out of getting it right?"

If you forget to include a biscuit, send a coupon good for dinner.

If you can't seat them together in coach, bring them to first class.

If you can't deliver in time, throw in something extra, and don't be stingy.

When you say you are sorry, be so generous that there is no doubt that you mean it. You will create so much word of mouth that your mistake will be worth its weight in gold. An occasional screw-up handled outrageously may be just what the promo doctor ordered!

Empower everyone to solve problems. Larry Okonek, director of training for PFM, a contract food-service company, likes to snack. He also travels quite a bit. He may be a good trainer, but he is a bit forgetful when it comes to packing for trips. That's how he came to be in search of snack foods and socks while on a business trip to Texas.

He stopped at a chain discount store and in a few minutes found two pairs of identical socks. He seemed destined for a quick in and a quick out. He was a little concerned to find only two of more than a dozen registers open. But no problem. The store wasn't very busy.

Then it happened.

The first pair of socks sailed across the scanner as the UPC bar code was read and the amount recorded. The second, identical pair (you guessed it) had no label. Then came the two most hated words in all of retailing. A voice that would wake the dead screeched, "Price check!" over the P.A. system.

Larry pointed out that the second pair was identical to the first.

No deal. Bar code or not, orders is orders.

The natives in line behind Larry became restless. Larry shifted from foot to foot. A native suggested that one pair of socks might be enough for a stranger just passing through town.

Larry considered. It's one thing to stand on principle. It's quite another to stand on principle in dirty socks.

Just when the situation looked as if it would deteriorate into physical violence, a scrawny kid with terminal zits appeared at the register and, yep, sure enough, same price as the first pair.

Larry was out the door before Miss Rocket Science could say, "Thank you for shopping at ————."

Across the street stood a bright, gleaming beacon in the Texas night: a Kroger supermarket.

Larry stopped and shopped, filling a tote basket with crackers, fruit, and cheese. He fell into line at the express checkout. Home free, almost (!), until the friendly cashier noticed that the cheese did not have a price tag.

Larry considered running. But before he could complete the thought, the cashier asked, "Did you happen to notice the price?"

"Two forty-nine, I think," offered Larry.

"I didn't think it was that high." She smiled. "I can call for a price check if you like. But would you like to take a chance that two dollars is about right?"

Imagine that! Someone had hired a cashier with brains and then actually given her the authority to use them.

This is a quiz: Where do you think Larry shops when he needs snacks? Kroger, of course. And what's even better is that they even sell socks!

We'll learn exactly how to empower your people in chapter 8, but for now, if you are in the business of selling socks, you'll know what to do!

Handle mistakes by the numbers. Having a system to handle mistakes is somewhat dangerous because it institutionalizes screw-ups. It may be saying, "We make so many mistakes that, rather than going to the root of the problem and seeking a solution, we'll just get better at fixing things."

Customers really are rather forgiving—once. But who would want to patronize a business that had to make mistake fixing a science?

We received an interesting printed card from one of our very slow-paying clients that read something like this:

"Vendors who do not receive payment within sixty days or who receive incorrect payment are invited to call our new problem-resolution line. Please leave a message and a problem-resolution clerk will get back to you within forty-eight hours."

We had a better way to resolve our problems with this client. We stopped doing business with them. Instead of fixing their system, they developed another system. How much faith could you have in this vendor's ability to resolve problems?

Still, you should have a system for resolving problems and responding to complaints. That system should focus on both resolving the immediate problem and preventing a future occurrence.

Every problem should belong to two people: the person directly responsible and someone with at least an impressive, weight-carrying title, preferably the owner.

When you know that problems that you create will come back to haunt you personally, you develop a totally different perspective on quality. This is particularly true when you know that both you and the boss will be charged with setting things right. Involving the boss in setting things right has several benefits:

- It lets the employee know that getting things right is important.
- It lets the customer know that getting things right is important.
- It lets the boss know about problems so that he or she can focus attention and resources on prevention.

Every problem or complaint should be documented, resolved, and, just to be sure, followed up.

Ask for the Customer's Opinion

Too many businesses still are not listening.

Rental car agents frequently ask, "How was your car?" They do this with their nose buried in the computer and a telephone stuck in their ear.

"Fine," I tell them. "It shimmies a little over ninety-five, but under ninety it runs great." Rarely does an agent so much as crack a smile or ask me to repeat myself. They just don't listen.

Serving outrageously demands that you develop your listening skills. Effective listening is more than an art. In the 90's, it will be the science of the successful. In chapter 6, we'll learn how to listen to your customers to discover opportunities to serve outrageously.

Promote Internally

"There is a surprising payoff awaiting these and other companies that imbue their customers with the service ethic: When they make customers happy, they make their employees happy, too. Contented workers make for better-served customers, and there is also mounting evidence that improvements in customer satisfaction lead directly to higher employee retention" (*Fortune,* June 1990).

As we will learn later, it takes a special personality to serve outrageously. But, special personality or not, you cannot focus all of your energy on the customer and expect employees to serve outrageously or even well simply for the paycheck.

We'll learn how to get ordinary employees to serve outrageously in a later chapter. For now, remember this: You cannot expect to wow the customer with knocked-out employees.

Know the Customer by Name

Everyone likes to see and hear their name. While your name is not who you are, it is the label under which you operate. Say the name of any famous actor and you immediately get a mental picture, usually accompanied by an emotional reaction. The same is true when someone hears his own name, particularly when it is used with respect.

Other than respecting a person's time as valuable, there is no greater way for a business to demonstrate status to customers than to know them by name.

Calling someone by name says, "You are special. I picked you out of the crowd. I remembered your name because you are important to me."

Winn Schuller, the late, great restaurateur from Michigan, was famous for his ability to remember names. Jane White of Houston recalls an evening when her father treated a group of twenty-five business associates to dinner at one of Schuller's restaurants.

Winn came over to the table and introduced himself to each diner. During the course of the meal, Winn checked back several times as he played his usual role of cordial host. Later, as the group called it a night, Winn stood waiting at the door, where he called each and every member of the group by name.

Does remembering a name make an impression? The story is over twenty years old, and it's still being told!

Make it a habit to learn the name of at least one new customer every day. Just walk right up and introduce yourself. This may be more difficult than you expect, but only with regular customers that you should already know.

A natural when it comes to meeting people, Don Bode struck up a conversation with a fellow passenger on a flight to Birmingham. As luck would have it, she turned out to be a regular customer at the chain restaurant that Don was going to visit.

On the following day, Don quizzed the crew about customer relations. Yes, they knew their regulars by name. Yes, the management made a special point of greeting everyone personally.

Then he described his seatmate, who just happened to have been a twice-a-week customer for more than eight years. And, no! They didn't know her by name.

Later that afternoon, their longtime customer and should-be friend arrived. Do you think it was difficult, after eight years, to ask her name? Of course it was. Outrageous servers don't wait eight years. They are like Winn Schuller, who considered you his friend in less than eight minutes and remembered your name to prove the point.

Invite the Customer to Play

If you really want to wow the customer, you must invite him to play. Positively Outrageous Service is Participation Service, and the trends favor those who reach out, touch, and involve the customer.

There are zillions of ways to play with your customers, if you are willing to be creative. However you choose to be playful, you are giving the customer a good dose of something magical—fun at an unexpected moment.

One day, after giving our manager his performance evaluation, he said, "I wish I could evaluate some of our customers!"

"Great idea!"

And we did. (See Customer Evaluation Form on next page.)

Sure, we give away a few meals, but only to our regular customers who were due for a freebie anyway. And think about the conversation when they get back to the office!

"How was lunch?"

"Great! I got my evaluation, and it looks like I need to improve."

"What?"

"My evaluation. I got my customer evaluation, and they said I was doing good but could use a little improvement."

"I don't get it!"

CUSTOMER EVALUATION FORM

Customer is: Orders:

_____ Regular   _____ Too predictable

_____ Irregular   _____ Eats like a bird

                                   _____ Eats lots of bird!

Miscellaneous:

_____ Please wash your car or truck. It's giving us a bad name.

_____ Please wash. *You're* giving us a bad name.

_____ Your bookie keeps calling here by mistake.

_____ Just what is it that you put in your tea?

_____ Is that your real hair?

While you're reading this, we're fixing your order, which is on the house today. It's our way of saying thanks for your business and for being a friend of _____.

                    Sincerely,

                    Scott & Melanie Gross, Owners

                    _____

                    Poultry Management Technician

Well, our customers got it. As one of them said, "You can eat chicken anywhere, but you can have a good time only in a few places."

Invite the customer to play. Remember his name, support causes he holds dear, be fanatical about product. Do these things and more, and your customers will leave saying, "Wow!" And when it comes to being top of mind, you'll be king of the mountain.

5

INVITING THE CUSTOMER TO PLAY—SHOWMANSHIP ON THE JOB

Showmanship is the art of giving products personality—yours!

"That's just what I've got! That's just what I've got!" shouted the hawker. His face was beaming and his pockets were bulging as he outsold competing vendors at least two to one.

What was his secret? Lower prices? Special product? Not at all. He simply drew the customer into the game with his cleverly constructed pitch. "Ice-cold beer!" tells you exactly what product is for sale. It's easy to reject without either looking or thinking. But "That's just what I've got!" invites the customer to look and then decide. In sales, looking is half the selling. The art of showmanship, whether practiced at a circus or an elegant restaurant, is indeed the art of drawing attention.

Frank Liberto was the National Association of Concessionaires' Showman of the Year a few years ago. But, in truth, Liberto is a showman every day. Maybe it's a genetic characteristic passed along from his father. But, whatever the source, Frank Liberto has more pizzazz in his little finger than most of us possess in our entire being.

He seemed an ideal source for a definition of showmanship. Oh, sure! The dictionary defines showmanship as "presenting an idea or product with pizzazz," a definition that catches the concept all right but fails to communicate the deeper meaning that true showmen express whenever an audience of one or 1,001 is about to be dazzled.

Late one wintry evening, Frank and I wrestled for an hour by phone until we finally had at least the germ of a more fitting definition.

We know intuitively that showmanship is the art of selling the sizzle and not the steak. But it was Frank who insisted that the showman's personality made the difference between simple marketing and true-to-form showmanship.

"It's the personalization of the products you sell," offered Frank. "If you think of your products as part of your family of offerings, it is much easier to personalize the sale."

Too dramatic, I thought. But definitely on the right track.

Frank continued that showmanship was not simply selling a bag of popcorn. It was a matter of selling "hot, fresh popcorn" with the added value of the seller's personality tossed in.

We tried again. "When you bring the character and personality of the individual together with the character and personality of the product, you have showmanship."

Better, but still a bit cumbersome.

Frank said that the personal involvement of the seller was the key we had to focus on. "If products can't qualify as a part of your own personality, you shouldn't sell them. Showmanship works only with products you believe in."

Slim sold novelties at San Antonio Mission baseball games. "That's just what I've got!" was his line. No matter what he had, the public turned to look. Then Slim turned his personality on to the product. According to Frank, "Slim wouldn't take out a poor product. It didn't have his name on it, but it had his personality on it."

We decided that personality is the key to defining showmanship. We also decided that a personality with a healthy dose of chutzpah was probably ideal.

"Passing a hot check is showmanship," Frank says. "It's just that the career is too short!"

We tried again. "Showmanship is the art of giving products personality—yours." (And it doesn't hurt if your personality is a bit peculiar!)

Showmanship is everywhere, and you don't even have to look because, done right, showmanship reaches out and snatches your attention!

"In the unlikely event of a loss of cabin pressure, oxygen masks will fall from the overhead compartment. Reach up, pull the tube to straighten and put on your mask as demonstrated. If you are sitting next to a child, or someone who is acting like a child, put your mask on first" (Southwest Airlines flight out of Dallas).

It was early on a foggy Sunday morning as a dozen or so weary travelers tossed first their luggage and then themselves into the National Car Rental courtesy bus for the expected boredom of a ride to the terminal at Chicago's O'Hare Field. Wrong!

A tall, lanky young man levitated himself into the driver's seat, adjusted his tie, turned up his smile, grinned into the wide mirror, and, using a P.A. system designed for monotoned announcements, shook the sleepy inhabitants of the bus back into first person.

"Gooooood morning, campers! Welcome to National Car Rental. And ain't this going to be the best day ever? In fact, it's early but I'm already . . ." And with that, he slam-dunked a cassette tape into a player that promptly spit out the Beach Boys refrain, "I'm picking up good vibrations. I'm getting those excitations."

The doors hissed shut, and the bus lurched forward as our driver-deejay launched into a nonstop commentary interrupted only by a medley of greatest hits from the 60's.

By now the passengers were awake, laughing and taking turns trying to outshine an obviously turned-on/tuned-in driver.

Suddenly both the bus and music stopped.

"Ladies and gentlemen, we are about to travel the most treacher-ous part of the parking lot. I don't know if the contractor was out to lunch or if he was an ex–navy man, but you are about to experi-ence 'the wave'!"

Without another word, only an ear-piercing war cry, our pilot whipped us at full speed over a parking lot that did indeed resemble the sea during a storm. We held tight and laughed all the way to the terminal.

Not one of us wanted to be first off and miss the rest of the best show in town.

HOOK, DEAL, CLOSE

Really good showmanship is often nothing more than jazzed-up salesmanship. There's a hook, the attention grabber that captures, perhaps demands, your attention. The hook is so different, bizarre, or funny that you cannot help but notice.

"That's just what I've got!" is a hook. So is "Ladies and gentlemen, welcome to Houston!" when it's announced by the flight attendant as your plane touches down in San Francisco! A hook is a head turner.

The hook turns into or sometimes is part of the deal. You could use the term "offer," which is gentler and more sophisticated. But a showman of the old school would be more comfortable with the term "deal." A deal is one of those "for you and you only—today and today only" propositions. You've heard it at the county fair just before you paid some outrageous price for a vegetable chopper or a knife you can use to either slice tomatoes or cut timber.

Funny thing about these deals: You know you're being conned, but it feels good so you play along anyway.

The last to come is the close. It's asking for the sale. That's when the carny at hand figures some clever means to get your head bobbing up and down and your wallet out of your pocket.

All showmanship doesn't have to involve money, even though you could easily ask, "Well, why not!"

Michael Hurst, president of NRA, has bugs on the menu at his 15th

Street Fisheries Restaurant in Fort Lauderdale. That's right—bugs! Hurst is a showman who nearly flipped when he heard about a shrimp-like seafood caught off the coast of Africa called "bugs." "I had to have it!" he said. And so, it turns out, do many of his customers.

A menu dish called "bugs" becomes a simultaneous hook, deal, and close for adventurous customers. Diners at 15th Street Fisheries have come to expect the unexpected. After all, this is the same place where a live cow was displayed for a month in the waiting area as part of an employee-created promotion. It is also where the entire Ohio State marching band paraded through the dining room at midnight one spectacular and very memorable New Year's Eve!

Bugs on his menu, some would say, bats in his belfry. And then there is the problem of all that cash in his registers!

ONE FOR THE MONEY, TWO FOR THE SHOW

We've said it elsewhere: Offering the customer an experience along with the product will be a significant competitive advantage. Why? Because technology and stiff competition make the 90's the decade of quality. Quality will be the rule rather than the exception.

Other than innovation, which will provide only the most fleeting of advantages, service will be the last frontier. Fortunately for the small business, the service advantage belongs to those who will think creatively and react quickly.

The good news/bad news of innovative service is that it is easily copied. Still, we've all heard the slogan "Often copied, rarely duplicated," which serves as a warning that creating opportunities for showmanship, which we could call "participative service," will not be enough. Managing others to serve lovingly, outrageously, will be the trick of the decade.

One for the money, two for the show, three to get ready, and go, man, go! What once was a cute way of starting a kid's game becomes a challenge to those who will serve Positively Outrageously. Get one for your money, the expected. Then get a second for the show, the unexpected. Showmanship is itself an unexpected added value.

Some have made showmanship an intrinsic, built-in, highly advertised part of the product, and that's fine. But, delivered as an unexpected bonus, a little "show" takes on even more value. Remember, the first principle of Positively Outrageous Service is that it is random and unexpected.

Knowing that you are always going to be well treated adds value and the excitement of anticipation. Not knowing how that good treatment will be manifested adds a sense of mystery.

County Fair, the amusement park mentioned in *Service America*, by Ron Zemke and Karl Albrecht, routinely self-evaluates its performance in the customer terms of friendliness, cleanliness, service, and show. Not a bad idea for a business that caters to customers actively seeking a good time. But then, what customer wouldn't enjoy being shown a good time in the course of any transaction?

QUALITY, ACCURACY, SPEED, AND SHOW

Any business transaction can be evaluated in terms of quality, accuracy, speed, and show. Give me a quality product, delivered exactly to my liking, do it quickly, and you've got a perfect picture of a well-oiled, efficient organization. But involve me in the process and make the purchase an experience and you've got the touch of showmanship that will make you more than outstanding—you'll stand out!

She wears a short, low-cut dress, mesh stockings, and black garters. How do I know? I've seen 'em, and so have the kids that secretly hope to join her performance at the bar. Did I say "kids"? Performance? Bar? You bet!

She's an old-fashioned saloon hostess at the Old San Francisco Steakhouse in San Antonio, where they know intuitively that a little showmanship is just the right ingredient to improve the flavor of already excellent steaks and seafood.

Each night, a young woman, clad in the traditional garb of an 1890's beer hall, climbs on top of the bar and perches delicately in a velvet-roped swing. A garter-sleeved pianist bangs out honky-tonk tunes as the hostess swings in ever-higher arcs across the bar. The bar itself must be thirty feet long, maybe longer. The crowded dining room grows quickly quiet as both musician and swinger increase their tempo. Finally, toe outstretched, the hostess rings a cow bell suspended from the ceiling at the farthest point in the swing's movement.

Naturally the crowd goes wild at this scene, which is repeated several times nightly every day of the year. Of course, we knew she would ring the bell, but, like the crowds at the car races, who don't really want anyone to crash, no one wants to miss the thrill of the moment.

At the Old San Francisco Steakhouse, the swinging hostesses further milk the moment by "trick swinging," if you could call it that, plus providing obligatory test swings to the several children who inevitably race to the end of the bar to watch.

Huge blocks of slice-it-yourself Swiss cheese further enhance what is only the merest hint that you're being naughty. After all, the ambience is of an 1890's bawdy house, be it ever so elegant. Besides, being left totally on your own to whack off as much of the twenty-pound block of cheese as you wish isn't much different from having free access to the cookie jar.

Quality food quickly served exactly the way you want it makes the Old San Francisco Steakhouse an excellent restaurant. But face it, excellent restaurants aren't that uncommon. But a girl in a velvet swing, well, that's entertainment. Just enough showmanship to keep the parking lot and cash registers full!

UNCLE BERGIE AND OTHER SHOWMEN

My grandfather was Uncle Bergie. No kidding! Grandpa was one of America's first deejays, spinning his 78's at restaurants and nightclubs throughout northern Ohio and Indiana on behalf of the Berghoff Brewing Company. Grandpa was one of an army of early showmen who "worked the boards" in the heyday of vaudeville, just before there were television and ad agencies (and before showmanship as an art form was nearly forgotten).

One of the early showmen was Donald Duncan, who in the 1930's elevated person-to-person marketing to a science. Duncan was fascinated by a Chinese invention, the yo-yo. But Duncan, who must have been an interesting person, studied the device and made a small but significant design change.

Duncan put a loop in the end of the string, which enabled the yo-yo to "sleep" at the bottom of its trajectory. This made possible any number of tricks. You remember—loop-de-loop, walkin' the dog, and, of course, rock-a-bye baby.

Duncan must have been puzzled by that old mystery of philosophy, "If a tree falls in the forest and no one hears it, does it make a sound?" Duncan wanted to make certain that the entire world heard about his invention.

There were other inventions and entertainments at the time. Probably some were more worthy of attention than a simple yo-yo. But working on the principle that it is indeed better to stand out than even to be outstanding, Duncan created a simple plan to make the Duncan yo-yo a household word.

(What plan do you have for making your product, service, name a household word?)

Duncan created an entire cadre of showboating, traveling hucksters who became modern-day Pied Pipers as they spread the word from town to town. They put on demonstrations, held contests, did anything and everything imaginable to create awareness.

They beat the drum so loudly that an entire generation of youngsters became hooked on what was no more than a pair of wooden disks and a short length of string. Hardly a kid in America grew up without owning at least one yo-yo. And everybody knew that owning a Duncan meant having the very best.

Today showmanship is alive and well. We just don't use the term because, thanks to the likes of Duncan and P. T. Barnum, showmanship came to be thought of as gaudy, tacky, definitely a quality of the beer-and-circus group. Who are today's showmen?

Airlines: Southwest Airlines

Southwest Airlines is nominated for making the serious and too often exhausting task of air travel fun with 737's painted like Shamu the Killer Whale, their twentieth-anniversary plane *Lone Star One* painted like the flag of Texas, and their willingness to throw a parade or party anytime an excuse can be either found or created.

(While waiting for the rough draft of this chapter to squeeze out of the printer, we opened the newspaper to the business section to discover this headline: "20 Years of Fun Have Paid Off for Southwest." We rest our case!)

Beverage Companies: Pepsi-Cola

Pepsi is nominated for having creative, involving promotions when by all rights they should be content to be a stodgy bureaucracy. They are also working hard to position themselves as more than a beverage company. They deliver more than soda; they also deliver service. And last but definitely not least, there's that dynamite commercial series, "You've got the right one, baby! Uh-huh!"

Cities: San Francisco

Where the mere act of walking from cab to hotel is an experience in audience participation, where there is always something different, low-budget, and personally involving to do. San Francisco is "Showmanship by the Bay."

Communications: CNN

For thrilling, live coverage in the opening hours of the Iraq war, CNN should be recognized for unexpected showmanship. CNN newscasters braved danger while other journalists played gin in the basement. They painted fascinating word pictures for millions of anxious Americans. Although they could leave only Peter Arnett in Baghdad, Bernard Shaw and crew mesmerized the world for a few thrilling hours.

Entertainers: Gallagher

Gallagher has to recognized for his topical humor that gets the audience into the act—and the act into the audience.

Entertainment: Disney

Disney is perhaps showman of the century for never being out of costume and for a fanatic dedication to a quality experience.

Food Manufacturers: Smartfoods

For marketing along the road less traveled and in the process becoming a cult food and a multi-zillion-dollar company, Smartfoods qualifies as the benchmark of corporate showmanship.

Religious Leader: Jimmy Swaggart

You don't have to share his religious beliefs to admire his sheer talent and showmanship. He plays the piano marvelously and sings—at the same time! He can preach dramatically and cry emotionally, also both at the same time. The man is a master performer.

Restaurants: Farrell's Ice Cream Parlour

For being first to literally beat the drum. Farrell's was early to institutionalize fun and motivate thousands of young people to play with customers.

Retailers: Nordstrom's Department Stores

Nordstrom's builds stores with a design that promises a shopping experience and then provides pianos, concierges, and salespeople to actually deliver on the promise.

WHEN TO SHOW AND WHEN TO GO

Showmanship isn't always appropriate. Sometimes customers do not want to play. They want fast, accurate service—nothing more, nothing less. The smart businesspeople know that the show should never interfere with or take precedence over the transaction itself.

In some businesses, the show is the transaction. Those are businesses where the customer is "in fun." In other words, the customer arrives expecting, indeed is paying for, a good time. But paying for a good time is not necessarily the same as wanting to participate personally.

I do not want to be the one the magician picks to bring on stage and have my underwear pulled out of a hat. But I don't mind watching it happen to you. In fact, seeing *your* underwear pulled out of a hat is a hoot! Just let me enjoy the action from the security of my seat.

So a word of caution to would-be Barnums: Not everyone wants to play. Some enjoy watching; others just want to get in and get out.

The Peach Tree is a tearoom in Fredericksburg, Texas. My Gran would call it "swellelegant." Beautiful, classical music and natural scented potpourri greet you when you enter the gift shop/art gallery that fronts the tearoom itself.

Once inside the casually elegant dining area, diners are presented with a choice of delicious, eclectic menu items, all fresh, all wonderful, and each beautifully presented.

A visit to the Peach Tree is an experience, reason enough for it to qualify as a provider of Positively Outrageous Service. But showmanship is still showmanship, even when it is subtle.

On one St. Valentine's Day, the co-owner graciously introduced himself to the guests and presented each lady with a fresh carnation. Just a small gesture, to be sure, but, oh, what an impact it made!

Some years ago, we took my youngest brother and my son, who are close in age, on a vacation. We had decided to make the trip a real adventure for the boys and chose every stop with that in mind.

For dinner one evening, we selected Bobby McGee's, one of the most entertaining restaurants anywhere. At Bobby McGee's, each waitperson dresses in a costume of his or her choice. In fact, it must be of their own creation because the costumes seem to fit each server's personality so well. (Notice how that relates to our definition of showmanship: adding personality to product.)

Our waiter was a magician. He amazed us with close-up magic, even juggling part of our dinner. The boys were truly amazed, having never seen such entertainment presented just for them, and at a restaurant, no less!

As youngsters often do, my kiddo had a sudden need to run to the bathroom, but he desperately wanted to wait for our magician to return to pick up the check. He was dying to both go and to deliver a funny line he had thought up all on his own. He wanted to ambush the waiter with "If you're such a good magician, why don't you make the check disappear?"

We laughed and waited. He waited and squirmed. Just when it looked as though he could wait no longer, our magician magically appeared and, with a great flourish, picked up our money. Before my son was able to deliver the knock-out punch, he leaned close, spoke first, and said, "If I were a really good magician, I'd make this check disappear!"

You can safely bet that someone visiting a Bobby McGee's, Disneyland, or a carnival is "in fun" and is fair game for institutionalized play. For the rest of reality, it is important to listen and watch for clues to the customer's disposition. Showmanship directed to individuals should not begin until the customer has responded to a friendly probe.

Start with a friendly greeting. If no sign of life follows, pass. Customers who show up in crazy tee-shirts or wearing "Kiss me, I'm Irish" buttons are telling you that it's okay to play. The customer who pulls into a quick-service restaurant drive-through and responds to a cheery greeting with "Give me a cheeseburger—and that's all" has made his disposition clear. Get him in; get him out.

There are exceptions.

"Gooood morning! Thanks for stopping by. Order when you are ready."

"Chicken tender snack and that's it."

"Yes, sir. That's a tender snack. That's it—and I won't even mention our fresh-brewed iced tea and sweet, buttery corn on the cob. Drive through and we'll have you out in a New York second!"

(At the pickup window) "What kind of corn did you say you have?"

"Sweet, buttery corn on the cob. (Smiling) Too bad I can't serve you any today. Maybe next time."

"I believe I'll try one."

"Sorry. You've already driven over the 'can't sell you more' line. Well, okay. As long as you don't tell anyone I was so easy . . . Might as well let me get you some iced tea to wash that down while I'm at it!"

It is possible to teach showmanship. It is even possible to teach showmanship to someone who has little or no natural desire to entertain. It's just not an easy thing to do.

To promote showmanship in any operation, you must:

- Hire showmen.
- Create opportunities for "show."
- Invite the customer to play.
- Reward showmanship.
- Be a showman.

At Macaroni's restaurant, the very talented staff will visit your table and absolutely knock you over with beautifully performed selections from well-known operas. This is a customer treat that could not happen without a crew that enjoys performing, never mind the talent required. Reluctant performers are not going to sing a cappella in a crowded restaurant.

Tableside opera wouldn't occur without the blessing—make that encouragement—of management. Management has to design the service experience so that that "performers" have both time and permission to entertain.

At Macaroni's, customers are not forced to play. You want opera? Ask for it. Unlike some operations that send musicians, palm up, to solicit table to table, Macaroni's is a class act. Customers may request a ringside performance or simply enjoy the moment when nearby guests are serenaded.

Showmanship unrewarded will not persist. What is interesting is that, for many, the opportunity to be "at play" with the customer is a reward in itself. Being at play is more than having fun on the job. It implies a sense of trust and freedom, something too infrequently seen in business situations. In fact, neither flamboyant showmanship nor gracious, subtle Positively Outrageous Service is likely to occur where freedom and trust have not been thoroughly established.

One additional element usually found only in an "in fun" environment is the costume. Costumes or masks have a way of working magic on both the entertained and the entertainer. Employees who may be reluctant to play with strangers (I guess their moms had something to do with that) will often experience an almost complete personality change when given the opportunity to perform from the safety of a costume.

Regardless of whom you hire or how you structure the job, it is unlikely that you will ever see employees inviting customers to play unless the boss leads the way.

The most fun airline in the sky, Southwest Airlines, got that way only through the leadership of Herb Kelleher. As proof, I offer the example of recruiting ads that feature Kelleher costumed as a rather poor Elvis Presley imitation and tagged with the headline "Work in a Place Where Elvis Has Been Spotted." (Interested folks who dial the 800 phone number are greeted with the Southwest "rap" hotline, a further sign that Southwest is a fun company looking for fun employees.)

On a smaller scale, the assistant at our restaurant learned a trick that could best be described as a bar-stool puzzle, one of those foolers that idle drinkers play on one another. He tried it on our drive-through customers, with great results. Wanting more, he approached with the suggestion that we teach any interested employee a simple magic trick.

I just happened to have with me an easy but mystifying trick called two-card monte. Within minutes, we had several budding magicians trying their new sleight-of-hand skills on delighted customers. In only a few days, their repertoire had grown to four or five, and several of our regulars had jumped into the act with tricks of their own.

Our manager often starts the day and the play by coaxing a smile from a slow-to-awaken customer with his magic. Even though the customers enjoy the magic trick, it is the humor and genuine childlike approach of the employees that make the moment. The line that always gets the biggest laugh is the one our manager delivers after he has dazzled one more surprised customer.

"If you liked that," he says and turns with a mischievous grin to our team leader, a grandmotherly sprite, "come back tomorrow. I'm going to saw Frances in half!"

All of our Christmas trees are adjustable . . . we have a chainsaw.
—Steven W. Gross

6

FINDING OPPORTUNITIES TO SERVE OUTRAGEOUSLY

It's too easy to say that your business is so predictable or conducted in such a high-brow fashion that there is no room for Positively Outrageous Service. Wrong. In fact, that kind of business is most in need of a little pizzazz to help cement the service event in the mind of the customers.

There may be more, but I can think of at least seven occasions when P.O.S. could be delivered.

1. Customers can be selected at random for special—outrageous—treatment.
2. Potential customers can be selected at random for special —outrageous—treatment.
3. Special events can be created specifically for loving on your customers.
4. Customer complaints or comments can serve as cues for Positively Outrageous Service.
5. While customers are waiting, serve them outrageously.
6. After the sale is the perfect time to serve outrageously.
7. Watch for serendipitous cues as triggers for outrageous service.

ERS CAN BE SELECTED AT RANDOM
CIAL—OUTRAGEOUS—TREATMENT

r anniversary and we were working in Austin. After a day of shooting video, we asked several locals where would be a special place for a romantic dinner. While none could agree on where we could find the most romantic atmosphere, when my wife mentioned her penchant for desserts, Pecan Street Cafe was the unanimous suggestion.

When the waitress brought the dessert menu we were overwhelmed by the taste-tempting choices. Everything looked so delicious that we each ordered a different dessert with a promise to share. The waitress was back in a flash with dessert, bringing coffee without being asked. You could call that good service.

The Italian cream cake was fabulous, but the huge wedge of chocolate-chocolate cake was too much for us to finish. Before we could ask, our waitress offered to package the cake to go. Now good service became great service.

At home the next evening we wolfed down our hastily prepared meal in anticipation of splitting the half-slice of chocolate-chocolate cake that we had brought home from Austin. In fact, we kidded about how we were going to split a serving of cake only half the size of either of our individual cravings.

Surprise! When we lifted the lid on the Styrofoam container, there was our leftover slice—plus a whole new slice!

Selected at random, we were the recipients of Positively Outrageous Service. We tell this story whenever someone mentions desserts, and we never stop in Austin without going for dessert at the Pecan Street Cafe.

A delivery customer at our restaurant seemed more than a little despondent when our cheerful assistant manager took her order by phone. A few moments later, as he was about to close the box, I happened to walk by and noticed a note in bold red marker written inside the box top.

"What's that?" I asked, expecting a silly explanation. Instead, he told how this particular customer needed a little extra cheer on this holiday evening.

I looked closer. The note read, "Merry Christmas from your *friends* at ———'s."

Rene McKee of the San Diego County Credit Union tells with professional awe the story of a Crocker Bank employee. Apparently, an elderly woman customer visited the bank on a regular basis and just as regularly confused her transaction. Noticing the lady's difficulties, a Crocker Bank employee arranged to visit the woman's home after work hours and balance her checkbook.

Other than the obvious value of doing a wonderful good deed, think of the word of mouth that such actions generate!

POTENTIAL CUSTOMERS CAN BE SELECTED AT RANDOM FOR SPECIAL— OUTRAGEOUS—TREATMENT

Mike Nosil, an executive of La Quinta Motor Inns and dedicated family man (not in that order!), remembers a trip to Nordstrom's in San Francisco on October 12, 1988. Funny thing about Positively Outrageous Service—it is always highly memorable. This event was no exception.

Mike and his wife are natural hand-holders who take time to smell the roses or, in this case, windowshop and browse through a newly opened Nordstrom's. It was Mike's first visit to a Nordstrom's, but now, after many Nordstrom's shopping expeditions, Mike recalls that this one was "a typical Nordstrom's, all brass and glass and, of course, a grand piano."

Mike was looking for a particular video game to take home to the kids. Being new to the store, the Nosils approached the concierge desk—yes, concierge desk—for directions.

"Instantly, two Nordstrom's employees materialized and asked how they could be of service."

When he asked about the video game, they explained that even though that was not an item sold by Nordstrom's, they had a computer that could help them locate the nearest dealer. Within seconds a print-out identified Macy's, a Nordstrom's competitor. So there they were not one but two Nordstrom's employees directing a potential customer to the competition. To make certain they found their way, the Nordstrom's folks reminded the Nosils to look on Macy's fifth floor. To make the experience truly outrageous, a concierge offered, "May I call ahead for you to make certain that the item you want is in stock?"

Not quite as outrageous but certainly something many retailers could imitate is our creative use of downtime for our delivery drivers. In the lull before lunch and dinner, we frequently dispatch drivers with boxes of fresh-baked, hot honey butter biscuits to local offices and stores. The drivers drop off a biscuit and, of course, a delivery menu to one or two employees. The result— sooner or later—is an order.

An Arby's manager tells a wonderful story about Domino's Pizza. With two teenagers visiting her home, the Arby's manager decided to surprise the kids with a pizza and stopped at the Domino's nearest her work to place the order and prepay.

The Domino's people informed her that the Domino's operation nearest her home belonged to a different franchisee. With a single phone call they placed her order and gave her the address of the delivering franchisee, who suggested that she drop her check in the mail at her convenience.

Good service, perhaps even great service.

The outrageous part came in the mail. Not only did she receive a personal thank-you note for her prompt payment, but enclosed were coupons for two free pizzas. Random and unexpected. Out of proportion to the circumstance. Highly involving, and, of course, the result was compelling word of mouth and lifetime customer loyalty.

SPECIAL EVENTS CAN BE CREATED SPECIFICALLY FOR LOVING ON YOUR CUSTOMERS

I walked into my restaurant and was greeted by a "Hello, Outrageous!" from my brother, Steve. "Let's do something outrageous today," he continued.

"Like what?"

"I don't know. It's your concept—think of something."

"Fine. Get some paper towels and window spray."

"The windows look fine."

"Not on our customers' cars! Hit the drive-through. You'll know what to do!"

For the next twenty minutes or so every car that stopped at the drive-through menu was attacked by a grinning manager armed with towels and window spray. From inside I took lunch orders, and from both sides we carried on an improvised repartee of gibes and jabs from "Your tubbiness" to "Mom likes me best."

"When that chunky kid gets out from in front of your car, drive through. No. On second thought, when he gets in front of your car, please drive through!"

"Please speak up. That's my older—much older—brother inside."

"With a shape like that, I'll bet he's cleaning your fender and hood while he's reaching for your window!"

"Don't listen to him. If he knew what he was doing he'd be out here!"

Usually by the time the customer made it to the window, lunch was ready and he was howling with laughter.

"When are you two going to start doing the insides?" a giggling lady asked.

"We're not. But tomorrow we're going to be offering hair-styling, and on Saturday we're going to try our hand at drive-through dentistry!"

With that the customers would shriek and ya-ha as they pulled into traffic. You can just imagine what the conversation was when someone at the office said, "How was lunch?"

Positively Outrageous Service events can be impromptu; in fact, some of the best ones are. But, if you are stuck for ideas, here's a system for creating an opportunity to serve outrageously.

- Decide when you can do something special without interrupting sales/service/quality.
- Decide when a P.O.S. episode will create the most exposure.
- Decide which customers will be most responsive.
- Brainstorm ideas.
- Decide who will participate.

Deciding When to Serve Outrageously

Of course, you can serve outrageously anytime. But it's doubtful, and not particularly desirable, that you would want to serve outrageously all the time. Remember, the first characteristic of Positively Outrageous Service is that it is random and unexpected. No matter how wonderful your service idea may be, it is the element of surprise that makes it special and spectacular.

Begin by looking at your operation and deciding when you could have an event so that normal sales, service, or production is not disrupted. Keep in mind that an event could be a single customer transaction or interaction. It doesn't have to be a major production.

Here's a favorite story supplied by Linda Cooper of First Chicago Bank. This story is most fun if you read carefully!

Heidi McCormack had just become a McCormack, and the couple had spent their wedding night at the Hyatt Hotel in Chicago before leaving for their honeymoon. The following night, when they were unpacking their luggage, Heidi's husband discovered that his pajamas were missing. Heidi telephoned the Hyatt long-distance and explained what had happened. The Hyatt responded that they would ask their housekeeping staff to look for the pajamas; if they found them, they would hold them until the couple returned to Chicago.

A week later, when the McCormacks returned from their honeymoon, they received a package that had been Federal Expressed from the Hyatt. When they opened the box they found the pajamas. The Hyatt had had them washed, pressed, and neatly folded. There was a note enclosed thanking them for spending their wedding night at the hotel. What's extraordinary here is that the Hyatt didn't make a mistake, the McCormacks did. The Hyatt seized an opportunity to provide P.O.S. and thus distinguished themselves in the McCormacks' minds (as well as those of all who've heard the story).

Decide When an Outrageous Service Episode Will Create the Most Exposure

Keep in mind that the whole purpose of Positively Outrageous Service is to create top-of-mind positioning. P.O.S. is a marketing strategy implemented one customer at a time. With that said, it is important to choose to do your good acts in public.

We'll take a modesty break to remind you that only healthy, profitable businesses will have the resources to serve their community. If your mission, like ours, is to "have fun and make the world a better place," then you must self-promote. Almost always there will be occasions when you do a simple good deed that should be kept private. But most of the time—promote, promote, promote.

If you intend to serve outrageously, do it publicly. Pick a time and place when you will be noticed. Remember, P.O.S. results in compelling word of mouth. What hasn't been said is that this word-of-mouth marketing can just as well come from someone who only observed as it can from someone who is directly involved.

Decide Which Customers Will Be Most Responsive

Some of your customers are shy, hardly noticeable. Others make their presence known an hour before they arrive. Usually, the outgoing, fun-loving individual will be your best P.O.S. target. That's usually, not always.

Extroverts enjoy participating in Positively Outrageous Service events. Better yet, they like telling about them. Since compelling word of mouth is the objective, they are the natural choice. Just make certain not to make two mistakes.

First, Positively Outrageous Service can be quiet and elegant, so you don't need to limit your attention to party animals. Second, that quiet, unassuming type may wield a surprising amount of influence, so think carefully before you eliminate candidates.

Brainstorm Ideas

Brainstorm ideas without limit to their elegance or bizarreness. The important thing is to get as many ideas as possible. Even stupid ideas can often be modified to become winners.

Get ideas from everyone and everywhere: employees, suppliers, customers, trade journals, and, most important, nonrelated businesses.

Here's a really dumb example—I love it!

Bill Behling from Beloit College strikes again. Bill offers his student diners the occasional invitation to a liar's buffet where everything on the menu sports a name other than its true label. Pinto beans might be labeled "giant caviar," and you can just bet that hot dogs are billed as "tube steaks." Fun, isn't it?

We do something similar when describing our honey butter biscuits. These babies are full of shortening. They're slathered with butter three times during the baking process and then drenched in honey just out of the oven. So what do we tell our customers with a smile and a wink?

"Ma'am, these biscuits have absolutely no fat or calories of any kind, provided, of course, you don't get them anywhere near your lips!"

Go ahead. Take any of the Positively Outrageous Service stories in this book and play with adapting them to your product, your operation. Keep these three tips in mind:

- Consider novel solutions to common problems.
- Consider things that a customer is likely to wear or display.
- Focus on the unexpected.

124

A participant at a P.O.S. seminar called recently and said that Positively Outrageous Service is just what is needed to put spark in her business. The problem: how to get started.

Here are some questions to answer:

- Do your customers need help installing or using your product?
- How do your customers arrive at your business: drive-through, walk-up, telephone?
- What could you do that would be considered out of proportion?
- What businesses share an interest in your success?
- What related businesses are good candidates for co-marketing?
- What local events, charities, or groups are candidates for an outrageous promotion?

Novel ways to use your product. Think. Is there something you could do to assist your customers in installing or using your product? Is there an interesting, perhaps fun way to package your product? Could you make a show out of delivering?

Novel ways to receive customers. Think. How do customers arrive at your business? Is there something unique that you could do to make waiting more pleasant? Can you think of something outrageous to do with parking or traffic arrangements? Can you make a game out of the purchase process?

What is "normal"? Think. What would be considered "normal" and how could you go overboard? If a restaurateur could earn your attention by serving a complimentary dessert, it would be of outrageous proportion to comp the entire meal. What kind of move would be comparable in your operation?

Who wants you to succeed? What suppliers have an interest in your success? How can they contribute expertise, facilities, product, or dollars to your Positively Outrageous Service plan?

Who else wants to play? What businesses share your customers but not your market? These make terrific co-marketing partners and may be found in areas you would never expect.

For example, we just approached a retailer of religious books to co-promote with our restaurant. They want the church business and—amazing grace—we do too! No conflict at all!

Discovering ideas for outrageous service to the community. Community service organizations need you. They are generally short on funds, facilities, ideas, and talent. Interestingly enough, you need them as much as they need you. Because community service organizations can deliver both the public and the media, devoting attention and resources to community service is an investment in which everyone wins.

Every business should subscribe to the local newspaper. If you are a business that is regional, national, or international in scope, the word "local" takes on an entirely different flavor. If you are operating a neighborhood dry-cleaning service, you need the neighborhood weekly and the city daily newspaper. If you are a manufacturer, your community papers are the *Wall Street Journal,* your association newsletter, and perhaps *Industry Week, Fortune Magazine,* and a few others.

Whatever constitutes "local" for you, it is your job to keep a finger on the pulse of your community of customers. Watch the media constantly for opportunities to get involved. Community service organizations spend so much time fishing for resources that they will be blown away when you call and offer to jump right into their boat!

Remember, though, that an offer to contribute funds will be first on their mind, even though it should be last on yours. When you call with an offer to assist or develop a benefit (make that "co-benefit") promotion, you should already have a good idea as to how you want to play. Your offer may be the use of your facilities for meetings or the loan of a special piece of equipment. If you have specialized talent, offer to lend expertise.

Keep in mind the firm promotional strategies outlined in chapter 4 as you screen the media for Positively Outrageous Service opportunities: Have fun, get people to your place of business, get people involved with your product, and, last but not least, do something good for others.

CUSTOMER COMMENTS AND COMPLAINTS CAN SERVE AS CUES FOR P.O.S.

In his book *Customers for Life,* Carl Sewell figures that a customer at his Cadillac dealership has a lifetime sales potential of $332,000. According to Carl, "You can't do enough for someone who is going to spend $332,000 with you." While it is not likely that every customer is worth $332,000 to you, when you put a pencil to it you are bound to be surprised at the value of even your most tight-fisted regular customer.

For example, a Baltimore-based credit-card operation calculates that it costs $100 to acquire a new card member. *Fortune Magazine* reports that "a five-year customer brings in an average $100 in profits annually, and a ten-year cardholder produces $300." It is unlikely that any customer staring at you across the counter is worth less than $100 per year.

How much would you spend to acquire a new customer? Well, then, don't be afraid to spend that much to keep one!

According to the U.S. Office of Consumer Affairs, between 37 and 45 percent of people who are unhappy with service do not complain. They go elsewhere. That's not the worst of it, when you think about the average of thirteen potential customers they will influence with stories about how poor their treatment was. When you think about customers in terms of both their lifetime sales potential and their impact on others, almost anything you can do to save a customer is a bargain.

Larry Okonek of Eau Claire, Wisconsin, tells about an experience with the tires on his company car. For the first full year, he regularly reported to the dealership for complete warranty service and preventive maintenance, which was to include rotating the tires.

Near the end of the warranty period, the dealer rotated the tires, and immediately the car began to shimmy whenever Larry drove faster than 60 mph. Back at the dealership, he was told that his tires were splitting and would qualify for an adjustment by the manufacturer because "we don't do tires." At the manufacturer's dealership, Larry was told that the tires were fine. They just hadn't been properly rotated.

When Larry picked up his car after another visit at the auto dealer, he discovered that nothing had been done. Instead, he was offered a pamphlet on proper tire rotation. "Wait a minute," complained Larry. "These guys were supposed to be rotating the tires all along. Don't tell me that improper rotation is the problem."

"I can tell you are upset, so we'll fix it, no problem."

With that, they simply rotated the tires back to their original position.

Larry figures that he lost maybe $20 in life expectancy per tire. But the dealer lost a customer for life.

My guess is that Carl Sewell would have replaced the tires and apologized for the slip-up. What would you have done?

Just plain good service that causes the customers to frequent your business twice as often will double your current sales without the need for a single new customer. Think about it. Customer frequency can dramatically improve your sales. You want to turn that volume up, and there stands an angry soul with the power to turn it off, completely.

An open market is a democratic market, where customers vote with their feet.

Here's a story of a problem correctly solved. In fact, because the problem was so well handled, we want you to know that it happened at First National Bank of Chicago, as described in the following customer letter:

> I recently experienced a problem with my personal checking account at FNBC as a result of some confusion over a bank policy regarding the availability of funds connected with a payroll deposit. The long and short of the situation was that not only did I misunderstand the bank's policy governing cash availability, but the teller who deposited my check and the first customer service representative I contacted

also seemed to be unsure or uninformed about the bank's procedures.

My first contact with customer service to answer my questions and
resolve my problem was entirely fruitless and frustrating. So I called
the office and an assistant responded in a concerned and caring
manner by putting my call through immediately to Gloria Marshall.

Ms. Marshall's handling of my situation was exemplary in every
respect. She listened to my concerns and responded with empathy
and respect. She initiated all stages of problem solving, including an
investigation of the bank's role in causing the situation to occur. Ms.
Marshall conscientiously called me as she uncovered additional information, and to follow up on each measure taken to resolve my
problem. I could not have been happier with the manner in which
Ms. Marshall responded—she made me feel like an important and
valued customer.

As a result, I am seriously considering moving my corporate savings,
checking, and tax deposit accounts to First Chicago. Despite the one
unhappy experience, I have the sense that if I ever needed help again,
Ms. Marshall and the FNBC customer service department are very
interested in building and maintaining solid business relationships
with their customers. And that gives me a lot of confidence in the First.

There is no better time for an out-of-proportion, unexpected response than when a customer is upset. At stake is that sale, the
customer's future purchases, and who knows how many other sales
that they can influence. A company can have a bad reputation—call
that positioning—even with potential customers who have never
set foot in the door.

A friend of mine lives just south of Austin, Texas. He recounted
for me his experience with a small neighborhood hardware store. It
seems that he attempted to return a small item, clearly marked with
the store label, and was refused because he had no receipt. This in
spite of the fact that the store owner/manager mentioned that he
remembered my friend's purchasing the item a few days earlier. A
customer also in line at the checkout stand overheard the owner's
refusal, pushed her full basket aside, and walked out, saying, "If
that's the way you treat this guy, I'm not going to give you a chance
to do the same to me."

By law, electrical parts cannot be returned for resale. Not far from the south Austin hardware store, the owner of a small auto parts store routinely accepts returned electrical parts for full credit. They go straight into the trash. For the wholesale cost of a set of plug wires or a turn-signal control, this sharp operator loses one sale but saves a lifetime of future sales and generates positive word of mouth.

Since many customers do not complain, it's only good business to have a system that encourages your customers to speak out. But even when customers do complain, it makes little or no difference if no one is bothering to listen.

Hardee's listens.

They listened when their largest franchisee, Boddie Noell, installed a toll-free customer response line. Dial 1-800-682-4590 and be pleasantly surprised when a cheerful voice with a soft southern accent answers, ready, willing, and able to solve your problem or pass along a suggestion or praise.

Hardee's corporate officials saw what was happening and weren't too proud to follow the lead of their franchisee. In some respects, they've gone one step further. Hardee's toll-free line is called the President's Hot Line. The very name tells the customer that someone important cares. Better yet, this number is staffed seven days a week, twenty-four hours a day.

The 800 number is posted by decal at the drive-through, on a special plaque at the counter, and, from time to time, on packaging materials.

Both corporate and franchisee systems employ pleasant adults and train them in Hardee's operations so they can deal with true understanding. They are also kept updated on company promotions as well as changes in the menu or operations procedures.

Jerry Singer, Hardee's director of public relations, says that customer complaints and, yes, suggestions and praise are followed up within twenty-four to seventy-two hours, depending on the nature of the call. The call records are computerized and forwarded by electronic mail to the president and appropriate corporate officers. Area offices follow up each complaint with a personal phone call plus a coupon for free product to make further amends.

Is it worth it? Well, besides listening to customers directly, Hardee's uses outside research firms to sample the feelings of Hardee's customers relative to a dozen or so attributes, such as speed of service, cleanliness, product quality, friendliness of service, and so on. According to Singer, and I think he is right, "It's hard to change someone's mind once they are fixed on how they feel about a restaurant."

Hardee's customer opinions are trending positive in every category. I think it's because they have managed to couple high-tech computer and phone systems with high-touch, love-on-the-customer, and get-things-right operations.

You don't have to be a high-techie to listen. MBWA, Management By Walking Around, applies to both employees and customers. But the only way to overhear a customer complaint is to put yourself right up front, where you can become an easily accessible target. You cannot run a business from the office. Get out there and listen!

Linda Fort, sales manager at the beautiful Y-O Ranch Hilton in Kerrville, Texas, overheard a customer complaining that room service was out of nonalcoholic beer, something that seemed especially desirable on that hot summer day. Fort apologized, dispatched the catering manager to the nearest supermarket, had several cases placed in stock, and sent a complimentary six-pack to the guest.

You can't hear if you don't listen. You can't listen from the office. Unheard problems are unsolved problems, and unsolved problems are lost sales. Period.

Customer Service Orientation

CARE Co., located in San Antonio, is one of the new-order businesses that will shape our service economy. Strictly Ma and Pa, CARE Co. publishes high-quality, customized newsletters and emphasizes service.

Jim Hayes, founder and co-mastermind of the company, selects new business much in the way you would expect his new clients to select CARE Co.

Jim looks for something he calls CSO—Customer Service Orientation. He says companies that only talk service aren't any better as clients than they are at serving the customer.

Jim and his wife and partner, Maggie, produce a newsletter body and then customize it for individual clients by adding employee news, contest announcements, and training tips. As a bonus, Jim creates custom responses to customer comment cards and then uses that data to shape future issues of the newsletter.

What is really interesting is the Hayeses' technique for preselecting new clients. First they try the product and service. Get low marks here and you are out of consideration. Maggie says that it was their intention from the start that CARE Co. be a business exclusively for winners.

She feels that ultimately any business lost because of CARE Co.'s selective pursuit of the best businesses will be offset by enhanced reputation and the lower cost of doing business with people who have CSO.

The next step in CARE Co.'s selection process is to, well, complain. The Hayeses feel that how their complaint is handled tells more about the potential customer than they could ever learn in a traditional sales call. Customers who respond with CSO are prospects for CARE Co. services.

Jim tells a story about Papadeaux's Restaurant in Austin. Known for good food, excellent service, and a fun atmosphere, Papadeaux's is the perfect match for CARE Co. Jim wrote a letter to the manager with a fictitious claim of disappointing food and indifferent service. (Here's where Jim starts to look a little sheepish.) Papadeaux's manager responded all right. He sent a letter of apology and a check for $30!

Whether you use the computerized data collection and shaping services of a leading-edge company like CARE Co. or something as simple as a customer comment card, it is absolutely imperative that you have a system for asking for the customer's opinion.

Tell Us

Only in Business Heaven is every employee a "10-percenter" (chapter 7 will explain). For those operating in the real world who cannot handle every customer personally, a customer feedback system is just what the doctor ordered.

But even something as simple as customer comment cards are a potentially dangerous method of gathering customer feedback. Handled properly, comment cards, or "tell us" cards, can become an excellent marketing tool. But the operating word is "properly."

There are four components of a properly handled customer feedback system:

- Immediate
- Top level
- Sensitive/action
- Extend offer

Customer feedback systems must offer immediate response to both the customer and the business.

To respond immediately, you must have the customer's name, address, and phone number. A serious complaint deserves more than a follow-up letter. It deserves a personal phone call.

Complaining customers are looking for a resolution of what they see as a conflict. They may want something fixed, an apology after slow service, or restitution for missing, damaged, or shoddy product. They want justice, and justice delayed really is justice denied. Besides, every hour that you delay in setting things right is another hour for the customer to stew in his anger, and another opportunity for him to tell someone else about how awful he's been treated.

Worse, a delayed response says, "We don't care."

One sunny February morning, I visited the offices of the company from which I hold a franchise. Spotting a huge pile of customer comment cards, I asked the secretary if any of them happened to be from my store.

"Don't know," she said. "We're too busy to do anything with them right now."

"Would you at least sort through to see if any belong to me?"

"We'll try to get to it."

On March 8, I received a comment card postmarked November 2. It was from a customer who had been shorted on his order. What do you think he thought about our operation? The obvious conclusion was that we didn't care.

If you care and want the world to know, then you must respond immediately.

Continental Airlines used to bill themselves as "The Proud Bird with the Golden Tail" and proved they were. Flights were on time, planes were clean and comfortable, and on-board service was both generous and gracious. Then something happened and all that changed.

In spite of marketing to the contrary, Continental became positioned as the "we don't care" airline. Nothing was more telling than the response I received to a letter that detailed a near-perfect return flight on Continental but also listed the problems encountered on the outbound flight, a flight that could have been a grade-B movie titled *We Flew to Hell on Continental.*

The letter from Continental arrived nearly sixty days after mine was sent. I had already chalked up their lack of response with an "It figures." When the incident was nearly forgotten, I received a reply from some junior, junior executive that made absolutely no mention of my lavish praise for the one really excellent flight.

Instead, he promised to pass along my criticism to the crew on the second flight. (Like I would care and the crew would understand the point of criticism delivered nearly two months after the fact.)

American Airlines did much better. They received these comments from an obviously pleased customer, Joe Jaeger of San Antonio:

> It was on this segment of my flight that I experienced the very finest service I have ever received on any flight, on any airline!
>
> This extraordinary quality of service can be attributed to the entertaining and highly professional manner in which your employee Mr. Robert Lager treated his passengers in our first-class cabin.
>
> I told Mr. Lager that his service was outstanding. He replied, simply, that he enjoyed and took pride in his work. Well, it showed!

> We all know how hard it is to find, and keep, good quality employees, and Mr. Lager is one asset that American Airlines can be proud of. He certainly deserves a "pat on the back" for doing his job so well and with such enthusiasm.
>
> It's service like this that keeps me coming back to American whenever my travel plans allow.

American responded almost immediately to let Mr. Jaeger know that his communication was both received and appreciated. They also promised that Mr. Lager would be personally commended for his fine service.

Communication to customers should be immediate and from someone with at least an impressive title. Both the quick response and the "high-level" respondent tell the customer that he is important. A sensitive response with a promise to take action tells the customer that you really listened.

Nearly every response should extend an offer of either a thank you for suggestions or compensation for slights, real or imagined.

Here are some simple suggestions:

Sample your product. Occasionally ask your customers to "try on" your product. Let them have a taste, a test drive, or some other small sample of your product and service in exchange for answering a few questions. Your customers will be delighted to help, and they will revel in the opportunity to be heard and have an impact on your business.

Include customer comment cards with every order. At least occasionally, include a customer comment card with every order, and make certain that they are conveniently available 100 percent of the time.

Post a direct phone number. Post the direct phone number of the manager or owner where customers can find it easily. The owner's home number is best, and you will be surprised to find that most customers will respect your privacy except in the most desperate instance, in which case you will want to be disturbed.

Call the customer. Whenever you can do so, without inconvenience to the customer, get a phone number. On a random basis, call and find out how you are doing. Most customers will be so delighted that you cared enough to call that they won't mind the interruption. When you call, know exactly what the customer purchased and when. This act alone qualifies as Positively Outrageous Service. It is random and unexpected. It is out of proportion to the circumstance, or at least it is out of the norm. The customer, of course, is highly involved, invited to share something very personal —an opinion.

Most service calls should be made by someone as high up the corporate ladder as possible. At least have someone say, "I'm calling on behalf of our owner" or some such status-bequeathing phrase.

No doubt compelling word of mouth will result. "I got the nicest call. Yes, the owner of Acme called just to check up on service. What a nice person!"

And, of course, such a call could contribute to lifetime buying decisions. Who wouldn't want to do business with someone who cares enough to consult you after the sale?

Broken Promises

An angry, red-faced customer bursts through your front door. You recall headlines of violent customers, berserk with anger, smashing store displays and managers who got in their way. Normal humans experience the fight-or-flight reaction that saved our prehistoric ancestors from being trampled by the woolly mastodon. But the truly outrageous manager just smiles and swings into action.

As Bill Oncken has said more than once, the best managers are in no way normal. They are as different from the normal manager as they are from the criminally insane. The same could be said about those who serve outrageously.

The best time, of course, to please the customer is on the first encounter, when their blood pressure is lower than 140/100. But if you must handle a customer who is beet-red and looking for a pound of flesh—yours—handle him outrageously. Positively Outrageous Service, even delivered well into the game, can save a customer, even create a customer for life.

A customer with a complaint has one basic thought: "Get this situation resolved and then I'll decide if you'll have another chance at my business." Negative word of mouth is the one power every customer can exercise. Sadly, they often forget to tell about those great experiences, but they never miss a chance to tell about how horribly they were treated.

Every product comes with a promise. Complaints are nothing more than a breach of trust, real or imagined. Your handling of a complaint must convince the customer that the slip was unintentional and that you are truly sorry, if not absolutely embarrassed. Leave the customer with an apology that implies you are only sorry to be caught and you've wasted your efforts. So apologize, and apologize big, for even the smallest broken promise.

A former West Coast resident, now an executive of La Quinta Motor Inns, visited Nordstrom's to purchase alligator boots for his wife's birthday. The good news is they had the boots. The bad news is that they did not have the correct size. The good news is that the salesman promised that he could, without fail, have the boots in time for the birthday. The bad news is that he was wrong.

On the day of the party, our friend received a telephone call and an apology. Two days later the boots were personally delivered by the salesman—at no charge for either delivery or the boots!

"Those were expensive free boots. Now whenever we go to the West Coast, we save our money so we can shop at Nordstrom's."

On a smaller scale, we have an arrangement with a local florist to provide us with small bud vases with a fresh rose or carnation. When we really, really blow it—and quite often just to say thank you—our delivery drivers stop in, pick up a bud vase and flower, and deliver it with a smile to our very surprised customers.

Broken promises are a test—of your integrity and of your willingness to set things right. As I researched this book, story after story involved Nordstrom's—not because they screw up more than anyone but because, when they do, they set things right, whatever it takes.

If you are tired of hearing about Nordstrom's service, then here's a challenge: Try to beat them!

Accentuate the Positive

Customer response systems do more than make it easier to complain. They also make it easy for your customers to make suggestions and to praise good service. You would be surprised at how many positive comments you can generate if you will just make responding easy.

At our restaurant, we put a customer comment card on every table. Occasionally we'll drop one in every bag at the drive-through, and we do random telephone follow-up on our delivery orders on a regular basis.

When we moved our comment cards out of hiding and began to actively solicit customer input, we were surprised at the number of positive comments. Today positive comments outweigh the negative nearly twenty to one.

Our customers feel more involved in the business. They seem to enjoy rewarding their favorite (and ours!) employee with their handwritten praise.

One customer suggested that several plaques that we had hanging on the wall should be moved from behind a plant. We moved them. Another suggested, to our embarrassment, that our dining room needed a fresh coat of paint. We painted.

But here is the really important point of customer feedback systems: They give you an opportunity to establish a personal relationship with your customers. To do this you must respond—*personally*—to every response, good, bad, or indifferent.

We write a personal thank you to every customer who takes the time to tell us how we are doing. And we send everyone a "be my guest" card good for a free order as a thank you and invite them to introduce themselves when they come in, to allow us to meet them personally.

You would not believe the people we meet at nonbusiness functions who say, "Oh, I know you. You sent me a letter once and a card for a free lunch!"

We have "be my guest" cards. In-N-Out Burgers in Los Angeles has a special coin good for a burger. The coins are so nice that many customers save them as collector's items!

Every business should have some small token that can be offered either to apologize or to say thank you. Every customer who bothers to tell you how you are doing should receive one.

WHILE CUSTOMERS ARE WAITING, SERVE THEM OUTRAGEOUSLY

There is no greater opportunity to offend a customer or treat a customer than a line. Customers usually hate lines, but it doesn't have to be this way. Understand the psychology of lines and it's simple science to turn a line into a competitive advantage.

First you must recognize several facts about lines:

- Lines are self-limiting.
- Lines can form only when customers arrive faster than they are served.
- Lines, once formed, persist indefinitely.
- Once service is delayed for any reason, every subsequent customer will wait for the length of the original delay.
- Lines are only as long as they appear.

Lines are self-limiting. There is a point at which people will no longer join a line. That point is determined solely by the perceived value of what is at the end of the line compared with the value of the line member's time.

Let's say there is a line and at the end of this line are crisp $1 bills. Each time you get to the head of the line you receive a single bill. How long would you wait in this line? If you would wait for five minutes, you value your time at $12 per hour. Would you wait an hour? And what if the reward was a crisp $100 bill?

People will join lines that stretch for blocks to board a spectacular Disney ride or attraction. They wouldn't normally join a similar line to purchase a hamburger. Obviously, many facts influence the perceived value of joining a line. How hungry you are for food or entertainment could have a dramatic impact on your willingness to wait.

In today's instant-gratification society, consumers are increasingly less inclined to wait. Businesses that can limit or eliminate lines have a distinct competitive advantage. If your line is long, your sales will be short.

In fact, long lines are definitely not a sign of prosperity, only of slow service. This is particularly true for businesses, such as restaurants, that experience heavy "rush hours." Such businesses actually turn away customers, having lost the sales advantage of being absolutely prepared for the first wave of customers.

Lines can form only when customers arrive faster than they can be served. Think about it. If a customer comes in and is served before the next customer comes in, you cannot have a line. A line is possible only if a second customer arrives while the first customer is waiting for service or to complete the transaction. Every time you see a line, you can be absolutely certain that at one time customers were arriving faster than they were being served.

Airlines and banks know about lines. Unfortunately, they don't know quite enough. They erect great, winding labyrinths of ropes and standards, and post elaborate electronic signs announcing which agent or teller is available. Why? Because they add extra service only *after* a line begins to form.

If they have enough employees available to keep the line from growing, then they have enough available to have kept a line from forming in the first place. If only they had had the employees up front and ready to go before the line formed, there would have been no line. Think how that would sit with the competition!

Lines, once formed, persist indefinitely. In the case of banks or airlines, notice that as long as management exactly balances the ability of the system to serve against the speed of arrival of new customers, the line will continue to persist forever. It cannot shrink because whenever a customer is served, a new customer takes her place. Whether the line is two or 102 customers long, it will never change in size.

Lines take on a life of their own, and people stand shifting from foot to foot as living testimony to management's lack of preparation.

Once service is delayed for any reason, every subsequent customer will wait for the length of the original delay. If ever there was an argument for original sin, then this is it. Let's say the world is unfolding perfectly. Every sixty seconds a new face walks in the door, makes a purchase, and turns to leave just in time to smile at the next customer. Now imagine what happens if you run out of merchandise and have to race to the stockroom, a round trip that takes two minutes.

Something is different, out of place when you return to the sales floor. Now instead of one customer there are two. Try as you might, you can only serve one customer per minute. Just as you bid one good afternoon, another customer steps into line behind the one waiting customer. You are doomed forever to face a line.

The interesting effect is that every subsequent customer must wait the two minutes you spent running to the stockroom. Theoretically this would continue forever, each customer paying in turn the price of your original sin.

Lines are only as long as they appear. People do not study lines. They take a quick look and make an instant decision. That's why you see snaking lines at Wendy's and you don't see them at Mc-Donald's.

Snaked lines are shorter than straight lines—at least that is the customer's perception. In the early 70's a major quick-service restaurant company developed what many thought was the world's most labor-efficient kitchen layout, capable of serving hundreds of customers an hour and requiring only a sparse crew of employees.

The design met all of its creative specs, except one: The customers hated it.

Customers were lined up in a single straight file. Even though the line moved very quickly, potential customers would see the one long line and instantly decide that, based on their experiences with quick-service restaurants, there was no way they could expect to be served from a line like that in less than six months! The design was abandoned.

McDonald's seems to understand that a customer would rather be number three in a slow-moving line than number nine in a fast line.

About that same time other restaurants decided that they could speed service and cut labor costs by installing a telephone at each booth or table in the dining room. Studies proved that both of the hoped-for efficiencies could be attained. Average time of service in one unit dropped from an already fast eleven minutes to an incredible seven minutes.

Again, the customers rejected what should have been an obvious improvement. Problem was, it wasn't all that obvious.

For dine-in customers, service begins the moment someone brings them water and a menu. In the traditional system this was accomplished almost immediately. Be seated, wait thirty seconds or so, and here come water and a menu. "Ah, we have begun!"

Under the new system, the first human contact, not counting your phone call to the order desk, wasn't until the order was delivered. Seven minutes.

The perception was that the service was slow, and, all studies and stopwatches aside, service always occurs in the customer's mind.

Here is where Positively Outrageous Service—or, more specifically, showmanship—can make all the difference.

Wait Not—Want Not

Making a wait pleasant or at least bearable requires a little creativity and just a touch of generosity. But be careful. Second-rate attempts often do more harm than good.

Think about the last time you waited in some dingy auto repair shop, drinking stale coffee, smelling like old smoke, and reading even older magazines. Makes a pretty good impression, doesn't it? In those cases, no waiting area would be a better plan.

Now here are a few examples of people who do it right:

Southwest Airlines. They remember their customers and treat them right on those early-morning occasions that roust them out for sleepy-eyed commuter flights. Southwest provides hot coffee and bakery-fresh donuts as a nice way to make waiting for boarding more bearable. And most Southwest gate areas are equipped with television to help you pass the time and keep current with the news or afternoon soaps.

United Artist Theatres and other forward-thinking chains play the latest previews on large color monitors to entertain and tease customers waiting for their show to be called. United Artists has done more than anyone to bring showmanship back into the theater, making an evening with United Artists more than a movie; it's an experience.

Wendy's. Here's a simple touch. Wendy's sends a smiling order-taker into the line in their dining room or at the drive-through to take your order in a pleasant and relaxed manner. Not only does it speed service, it creates a perception that the service is even faster. An added benefit is that customers don't feel the pressure of the line behind them and can take their time deciding.

Marriott. Probably the best at paying attention to waiting customers, called "guests," Marriott is quick to offer juice or fresh fruit to guests waiting to check in or out.

Alamo Cafe. Here's an example of an independent restaurant that has moved production into public view. In this case, fresh, chewy flour tortillas are rolled, pressed, and grilled right before your hungry eyes.

The Olive Garden. Waiting at the Olive Garden is almost as good as the meal. You get to people-watch while friendly employees circulate with baskets of straight-from-the-oven breadsticks . . . ummm.

Macaroni's. Here's an independent restaurant that has turned waiting into an art. Careful, don't arrive before the dinner rush, or you'll miss the pleasant wait that leaves you to wander through a gorgeous Italian deli where you help yourself at a casual wine bar. Be careful to keep track of your refills: At Macaroni's it's strictly the honor system when it's time to pay up.

AFTER THE SALE IS THE PERFECT TIME TO SERVE OUTRAGEOUSLY

To me it was just a nice pen. Big, fat, and trimmed in gold, with a peculiar white top. It rode well in a shirt pocket for business or clipped inside a tank top for working on the property.

And then it happened. A yuppie friend visiting for dinner did a double take and reached toward my chest. "Ah, a Mont Blanc." At first, I thought he was about to brush off a bug. Instead he pulled out that nice, big pen, which had been a gift.

"It's a Meisterstück," he marveled.

"A meister what?"

"A Meisterstück—you don't know what that is, do you?"

"Of course I do," I snapped, remembering at the same instant what Mom had said about lying and Hell.

That's how I discovered Mont Blanc. A close examination and the peculiar top made sense. Mont Blanc, white mountain.

And then you begin to notice that Mont Blanc owners sometimes accord one another a certain respect without thinking and that, when asked, nearly everyone admits that the pen was a gift.

You can imagine what it's like to be working at our restaurant and have a drive-through customer ask to borrow a pen. My first thought is panic as I look everywhere to find them something cheap to write with. Then I begin to feel embarrassed. What the heck! It's only a pen. No, it isn't! It's my Mont Blanc!

So I offer the pen and stand there, eyes riveted on my pen. The building could fall down around me, and I still wouldn't lose sight of that pen!

Mine served me well until one warm spring afternoon. While I was taking a very large order, my Mont Blanc died. I nearly followed suit.

"My Mont Blanc," I wailed, as my brother tried to encourage me to focus on the business at hand. It was at an odd time when you couldn't find a Mont Blanc anywhere at any price. Thoughts of my banishment from the Mont Blanc fraternity created a mild panic.

Then I thought, "Boy, this is an expensive pen. I bet they'll fix it!"

Within hours my pen was wrapped and bundled for shipment to the Mont Blanc service center in New Jersey. New Jersey! You've got to be kidding! Why, there's no telling when or if ever that pen would come back.

I removed the refill.

Okay, so that makes me cheap, distrustful, you name it. But a Mont Blanc refill costs $4, and I have suits that aren't worth that much.

I waited what seemed like months, left to get by using a mortal pen. The ten-day wait took forever.

Then it arrived. I ripped open the package and, yep, there it was, my beautiful Mont Blanc! Click, click. It worked. Good service!

Click, click. What's that? A new refill? They didn't steal my pen! They gave me a new refill! Great service.

Click, click. What's that? Well, I'll be darned. They reengraved the barrel. There it was—S.G., just like on the barrel that had cracked. Positively Outrageous Service. And at absolutely no charge.

One of the best times to serve outrageously is after the sale. This is a time when a customer may not be certain about his status. After all, you have already parted a fool and his money. That's why a personal thank you note or a telephone follow-up takes on extra meaning. You don't have to do it. There is no additional money in it for you. You must genuinely care. Amazing.

Mike Nosil, an executive of La Quinta Motor Inns, returned to Nordstrom's to replace a pair of shoes he had purchased a year and a half earlier. He told the salesman that he had enjoyed the old pair, but that they were not as comfortable as he had expected.

"What are you going to do with the old pair?"

"Well, since they are so uncomfortable, I'll probably toss them."

The salesman inquired further about the shoes and their fit. He then explained that one new style sold about one and a half years prior had since been redesigned to correct the fit problem.

"Why not return them?"

"I'm from out of town, and they're at my hotel."

It turned out that the hotel was near a different Nordstrom's.

"I'll call a friend in that shoe department and let him know that you are going to return your shoes."

Later, at the second Nordstrom's, the salesperson said, "I think these shoes originally sold for about $165. Will a credit for that amount be okay?"

Service after the sale adds unexpected value to the product.

To me a Mont Blanc pen is a bargain. If mine were lost this morning, make no mistake about who would buy a replacement this afternoon.

To Mike Nosil, you can bet that a product purchased from Nordstrom's had more value than that same product purchased elsewhere.

WATCH FOR SERENDIPITOUS CUES AS TRIGGERS FOR OUTRAGEOUS SERVICE

You never know when an opportunity to promote or serve outrageously will arise.

> Manager, watching the garbage man do his thing: We're probably the only people on earth with a boring title. Even the garbage man is called a sanitation engineer.
> Owner: So what do you suppose the city would call your job?
> Manager: Poultry management technician.
> Owner: Get new name tags.

Or take Lambert's Cafe, described in chapter 2. The story goes that one busy day, a Lambert's customer called from across the room that he wanted another roll.

"Be with you in a minute" was the gist of the reply.

"Aw, just throw me one."

And a legend was born. All because someone took advantage of a very tiny window of opportunity.

146

How about this one? A customer comes into your store, gathers her purchases, waits in line, and, upon reaching the checkout, discovers that she left her wallet at home. What do you do?

Well, at our place we say, "No problem. Your food is hot and ready. Next time you are in the neighborhood you can take care of us." Ten times out of ten they are back within the hour.

Sure, we could hold their order under the light and send them to the nearest ATM. But why add hassle to embarrassment? The risk is minimal, and the potential for compelling word of mouth is considerable.

Here's a better one. Larry Okonek, who has shared other favorite stories, tells this one.

While in Montreal, his conference group organized a dining adventure to a place called Sugarhill's. Larry says that Sugarhill's is the ultimate outrageous restaurant because the entire experience, not just the food, is designed to involve the guest.

From the parking area, guests are treated to an old-fashioned buggy or sleigh ride, depending on the season. Employees in traditional garb cater to the diners' every whim. But here's the interesting part: You've seen commercials that advise you to carry Visa "because they don't take American Express"? Well, at Sugarhill's they don't accept either. It's cash on the barrel head. What, no cash? No problem. They give you a business card and tell you to drop a check in the mail when you get home!

You can find opportunities to serve outrageously in the most unexpected places. Midwest Express Airlines found their opportunity under a seat!

Lucy Harr, senior public relations officer for the Credit Union National Association, wrote to brag about her treatment while a passenger on Midwest. It seems she lost an *E* from a travel Scrabble game while playing en route.

"When they noticed that I was searching for something, the flight attendants asked if they could help me find it. Since it was time to get off, I left my business card and a request to send the *E* if they should find it. I fully expected my card to be tossed and the incident forgotten. Imagine my surprise when I received an envelope later

147

that week with an *E* traced on the outside, a pleasant note from the entire crew, and my missing *E*.

"I've been more impressed with this incident as time passes because my colleagues and I have left other things on airplanes and never been able to get them back."

Opportunities to serve outrageously are yours for the taking or for the making. All you need is a fertile imagination and the willingness to listen. Listen to your community. Listen to your customers. And it won't be long before your customers will be your sales force and even your complainers will be customers for life.

Once you earn a negative position in the mind of the consumer, it is extremely difficult to regain the consumer's confidence. It would be less than honest not to report that Continental is working hard to make a difference.

Here's a story that should prove the point.

On a recent flight from Houston to Dallas, a delay of one and a quarter hours was announced. The Continental gate agent arranged for snack service, soft drinks, and peanuts so passengers could have something to eat during the delay. This was not a scheduled meal flight and it was at 8:45 P.M.! Once on board, complimentary cocktails were offered. Again, this was not a necessary service but one done out of genuine concern and courtesy for each and every passenger.

Continental's ads promise "One airline *can* make a difference!" Looks like they mean it.

Just to prove the point . . .

Southwest Airlines may very well be the country's premier example of institutionalized Outrageous Service. You could easily fill a book with Southwest stories. We'll just round out a chapter!

"Frequent flying to my mother and aunt is twice in seventy-four years! They were worried about missing their connections and the confusion they might encounter in the process.

"Sonja recognized the problem with two inexperienced senior citizens attempting to travel on their own. Sonja then *volunteered to escort them to Little Rock* the next day since it was her day off. This offer to help my mother and aunt took me by surprise. Sonja did arrive as promised and took care to see that my mother and aunt made their connections in Little Rock.

"Southwest should be proud of such considerate and dedicated employees as Sonja. Employees like her can only help build the image of a company."

Joy and Lynell were walking through the Love Field terminal when they passed the shoeshine stand, where a gentleman was getting his shoes shined. Lynell saw the gentleman and stated, "Hey, it's good to see your face again." His reply to her was "Yeah, yours too. By the way, *thanks for the phone call.*"

Joy asked Lynell about the phone call, and she explained that 'the gentleman is one of our regular customers' and that she had not seen him in a couple of weeks. So, being worried that he might be ill or something, she called his office to determine if he was okay. The gentleman got on the phone, laughing, and thought it was a real "hoot" that she called to check on him.

"You might be asking yourself why I'm bothering to write this letter to you. *I want to say thanks for running the most consistently fun and friendly airline I have ever been on.* All too often, while immersed in busy schedules, it seems people can always find time to complain about something. Not often enough do people take the time to say something nice. Southwest is number one when it comes to making people feel good about flying, and I look forward to every trip.

"I am based out of Austin, and out of the two airlines that I fly the most, Southwest again comes out on top with respect to quality of service, consistency, and friendliness. It is a fabulous feeling to have a smiling ticket agent greet you with the words 'Good morning, Mr. Marek' without first looking at the name on my ticket. The other airline greets me with 'May I help you, sir?' no matter how many times I deal with the same ticket agents.

"The early-morning Austin staff is really first rate. There are, however, two individuals in Austin that stand out above the others. Anita

149

and Jody are always smiling and always a pleasure to deal with no matter how late I'm running trying to catch the 6:40 to Dallas. It's a great way to start my day with such pleasant people."

"Here's what happened (it's kind of a long story but it's a good one).

"I arrived at Sky Harbor to find that my flight home to San Francisco had been delayed indefinitely due to bad weather in another city. Like the other passengers, I was not pleased and I dreaded the thought of being stuck in a crowded airport for hours.

"A quick look at the video monitor showed another flight to San Francisco via San Diego. I asked Sherri if she could put us on that plane; she said she could and did so. Ten minutes after we left the ticket desk, happily rerouted, my girlfriend noticed another nonstop flight to Oakland that would be more convenient for us.

"Could we switch again? We had already changed our tickets, our luggage was gone, and the airport was a zoo filled with cranky travelers. I got back in line to speak with Sherri again.

"She told me she could change our tickets but that it was uncertain if the luggage would make the new plane assignment. If it didn't, she explained, we would have to pick up our bags at the San Francisco airport. I told Sherri that neither of us had a car and that it would be difficult to go to SFO to get our bags. I asked if there was a way to know if our bags made it to the new flight.

"Here comes the superhuman part. Sherri told me that she was about to have a break and that she could take that time to retrieve our luggage personally. The next thing I knew, Sherri was getting approval to go into the secured luggage area, and within fifteen minutes, she came back smiling. 'Everything's okay,' she told us.

"At that moment, two things struck me deeply. First, I was amazed that anyone would sacrifice their break to hunt for our bags amid the tons of luggage in the airport loading area. Second, I was humbled by the thought that it was my fault that she was burdened by two successive reroute requests from the same travelers. Third, I was impressed that anyone could remain so cheerful, especially during the hectic holiday travel season."

150

"One of the stewards was a regular Rodney Dangerfield, cracking jokes and making everyone laugh. I'll have to admit, I have never seen so many people in an aircraft pay that much attention to all the preboarding announcements and safety features that, for the most part, are rarely listened to.

"He referred to the emergency floor lighting as 'that snappy disco floor lighting,' warned people that if they were going to smoke on board they would be escorted outside at 25,000 feet for a very special presentation of *Gone With the Wind,* and when it came time to collect all the beverage glasses, he sang, 'Stop! what you're drinking now' to the tune of 'Stop! in the Name of Love' by the Supremes. And this all took place on *Lone Star One,* the Boeing 737 jet painted like a giant flag of Texas. What a trip! We all gave him an ovation, and I personally never knew flying could be so fun!"

7

SERVICE—AN AFFAIR OF THE HEART

Every manager should know by now that what the customer really wants is service. Personal service, the kind that is delivered by live bodies behind the sales counter, a human voice at the other end of the telephone, real folks in the teller's cage at the bank.
—*Patricia Sellers in* Fortune Magazine

The men and women on Madison Avenue know what turns on customers. They produce the commercials and ads that fill the airwaves and print. Now here's a test. Think of three recent commercials. Go ahead. Write down the names of the companies, just so you don't cheat. Question number one: How many of the three featured items do you really need? Question number two: How many of your commercials featured a price?

Most likely your answers were zero and zero.

Why? Because most of the really effective commercials produced today are for items you don't desperately need. And price is rarely mentioned. Even in the age of discounting, Madison Avenue knows that we rarely buy on price. Instead we buy an opportunity to feel good.

Glynn Barclay checked into the Marriott in downtown Washington, D.C. He wasn't feeling well, and he certainly wasn't happy with a room rate that to his way of thinking was exorbitant.

A couple of days later, Glynn awoke with a monumental problem with his throat. He called the Marriott operator and asked her to recommend a doctor. Good service would have been for her to give Mr. Barclay the name and number of a nearby doctor. She refused. Well, not exactly refused—more like insisted that she help by personally locating a doctor.

"Mr. Barclay, we will contact a doctor as soon as possible, and I'm sorry you are not feeling well."

Within two minutes a sharply outfitted security officer was at the door.

"Hello! Is there anything we can do? We understand that someone in the room is not feeling well."

Barclay thanked the officer for his concern and said that the hotel operator seemed to have the situation under control.

"Well, we're terribly sorry, and if you do need us, just call and we'll be here immediately. Don't be embarrassed or hesitate to call. We're here to do whatever is necessary to make your stay as pleasant as possible."

Within minutes the operator called to report that she had called for a doctor and gotten a recording. She promised to keep trying.

Every fifteen minutes or so, in spite of the early morning telephone traffic, the operator called to check on her guest and remind him that he was her top priority.

At 8:10 A.M., the doctor's office called.

When Barclay returned to his room later that evening, he noticed that the message light was on. It was from the morning operator. She had called from home to make certain that her guest was getting plenty of that Marriott world-class service.

According to Barclay, "Long after I forget how much I paid for the room, I'll remember how I was treated and how I think that they really cared. The next time I'll know that, at any rate, I'm getting a bargain."

SERVICE IS AN AFFAIR OF THE HEART

In *Future Perfect,* Stanley Davis says it like this: "Intangible services are performed in addition to being produced. They are essentially social actions conducted between the deliverer and the consumer."

Okay, Mr. Davis, you are correct. But the Disney people are a little closer to the truth. Ask them how they select employees and they'll do something that is at first confusing. They just smile at you and say nothing. Then it strikes like Zen lightning. Aha! It is important to hire people with nice teeth. Of course, that's not their answer at all. Disney looks for people who smile.

And that's not bad thinking. After all, if someone isn't smiling during the interview, what in the world would make you think they will be smiling when faced with a line of customers all in a hurry for service, service, service!

Let's get right to the truth: Service is an affair of the heart, because for service to touch the mind of the consumer it must come from the heart of the server. As Sally Field once said at the Academy Awards, "You like me, you really, really like me!" And that is the exact reaction that people feel when they are served outrageously.

Donald O. Clifton of Selection Research, Inc., impressed me forever when he spoke at a National Restaurant Association show in the late 70's. According to Clifton, you can evaluate your business in the traditional terms of profit, inventory, turnover, return on investment, or any one of a dozen standard accounting measurements. But why not, he asked, evaluate your business in terms of the customer?

Clifton suggests four customer-focused measurements of business success:

- Awareness
- Preference
- Frequency
- Feel Good

First, there is awareness. This is the percentage of your market that is aware of who you are, what you do, and perhaps a little about your operation, such as location, hours, and special services. The higher your awareness, the healthier your business. After all, you are not likely to do business with someone who doesn't know you exist!

The second customer-focused measurement is preference. This is simply the percentage of potential customers who would, when given a choice, choose your product or service over that of a competitor. "Do they like you? Do they really, really like you?" (Shut up, Sally!)

Measurement number three: frequency. How often do your customers repeat? This measurement takes on different meaning depending on the business you are in. Obviously, if you are in the business of selling refrigerators, if a residential customer comes in once a month you've got a problem. On the other hand, once-a-month frequency for a fine dining restaurant would be terrific. Just as once-a-month frequency for a dry cleaner would be awful.

Clifton's final measurement is called relationship extension. I call it Feel Good. Whatever the term used, we want to know how many customers are recognized personally. "Good morning, Mr. Smith" is fine, but "Hi, I see you got your Chevy running" is nearly as good. A smile and friendly, personal greeting is a sign that the offer of a personal relationship has been extended, an attempt made to make the customer welcome, to Feel Good.

You can test yourself against Clifton's measurements. Venture into your market. Ask at random about your business. If they can tell you about your company, perhaps give you directions to the location, or recommend one of your services, then give yourself a point. If when you mention your company's name the only response is a blank stare, start to worry.

It's not reasonable to expect everyone to be able to express awareness about your business. Not everyone may be a potential customer. And there are those who inhabit the earth but live in another dimension. These folks you can discount with confidence. Still, if you aren't batting at least 90 percent among your potential customer base, you need more work toward that top-of-mind position.

Wander into the world with a coupon good for something wonderful at your place and a similar goody at your competitor's. Offer one or the other to a potential customer and you'll know in an instant who is perceived as the best in your business. Score less than about 75 percent and you've got some serious work to do.

The rest of the survey can be conducted from a chair in your place of business. Start by asking how often they visit. Almost every industry has a standard for customer frequency. If you don't know yours, ask your industry association leadership; they do know.

To study Feel Good, just sit back and watch. How many of your customers are greeted by name or in some other manner that would indicate that they have been personally recognized? The higher your industry standard for frequency, the higher the percentage should be of customers recognized by name.

Every business has its regulars. You should be no different. Regulars should most definitely be recognized by name. If you don't recognize customers, members, patrons, or guests, at least have the good sense to create a system for finding out early in the sales process so you can refer to them by name thereafter.

As important as a name may be, it's not the be-all/end-all of Feel Good. Watch for those subtle signs that indicate that a customer is receiving personal attention. General playfulness is a great sign that Feel Good is in the air. It is also the leading indicator of willingness to serve outrageously. Joking with your customers creates Feel Good because the natural assumption is that you wouldn't "play" with someone you don't like.

> Employee: I'm sorry, ma'am. There will be a thirty-second wait on your fried chicken.
> Customer: (At drive-through) No problem.
> Employee: Well, I need to warn you that it's going to be even hotter than usual. In fact, if you bite into it too soon, your lips will fall off.
> Customer: I'll be careful!
> Employee: That's what they all say. But then they look in the box and it looks so good and the smell just jumps right out at them and boom! Before you know it—lips all over the drive-through. No problem for us, though. We just sweep 'em up and sell 'em for bait!

Before we miss the point entirely, notice the relationship between frequency and Feel Good. You can double your business without a single new customer if you make your current customer base feel so good about doing business with you that they come in twice as often. Before you make a list of all the places where this concept does not apply, make a list of all the places where it will. Give me a call sometime in the next century when you finish.

Feel Good creates word of mouth. Feel Good is at the playful heart of Positively Outrageous Service. Feel Good comes from the heart.

The problem is that not everyone wants your customers to feel good.

SINGING PIGS

"Never try to teach a pig to sing. It wastes your time and it irritates the pig." That's the way I seem to remember Clifton saying it.

A pig farmer in Lampasas, Texas, had a different version: "Never wrestle with a pig. You get dirty and the pig loves it!"

However you say it, not everyone is psychologically capable of extending Feel Good to perfect strangers. No matter how much training, incentive, or innovative job design you offer, you are absolutely wasting your time on those whose psyches just won't allow them to get lovey with a customer. Not only are you wasting time, money, and effort, you are probably irritating the heck out of them!

Some people have difficulty being warm and friendly with their spouse. And no, I am not calling them pigs, that's just an example. You could just as easily cite the saying "You can't change a leopard's spots."

We walked into a theater, my client and I, and were greeted by a dour-looking doorman at the ticket drop.

"Your theater is to the right," he moaned.

"So what's with Mr. Excitement?"

"Oh," said the client, "that's Harry. He's a little different, but after a while he grows on you."

"Mold will grow on you. But I don't think I would hire it to greet my customers."

The American economy is increasingly a service economy. By the

157

year 2000, some 92 percent of all U.S. employees will work in a service industry and account for 85 percent of the gross national product. Here's a pop quiz: True or false—IBM is a manufacturing company. If your answer is true, try again. In 1990, IBM had nearly 400,000 employees worldwide. Only 6 percent (about 20,000) were involved in manufacturing.

The trend toward a service economy means that every day we are becoming a nation of first impressions. Our daily lives are a series of pop quizzes, instant decisions about whether or not we like a product or service. There's an old saying: "You never get a second chance to make a good first impression!"

The point is simply this: The successful business of the 90's will neither recruit nor hire employees who do not make a dynamite first impression as they go about the business of making customers feel good.

FINDING FEEL-GOOD FOLKS

Success in the 90's will depend largely on the *r* words: recruiting and retention. In a later chapter we'll look at how to hang on to winning employees. But first you must find them.

How to Hire Lovers

Ed McGowan of Bryan, Texas, headed for his parked car. Being something of a neatness fanatic, rather than ignore a piece of trash he stooped to pick it up and drop it in a nearby dumpster. Ed was surprised to discover that his trash turned out to be treasure.

Falling from what at first appeared to be a discarded envelope was a $100 bill. Attached to the currency was a bill from the electric utility. Also enclosed was a note obviously written by an elderly woman telling how much change she expected.

McGowan, like a retail Will Rogers, has never met a customer he didn't like. He even loves the customers he has yet to meet. Unable to contact the owner of the missing $100, Ed paid the bill to prevent a cut-off of service and took both change and receipt to the police department.

Security experts tell us that 5 percent of the population are pathologically criminal. Some 85 percent of the population are basically good, provided that they are not faced with a situation that makes misbehaving risk-free. The remaining 10 percent are the saints of the world. They rarely have second thoughts about following the golden rule. They are the original doers-unto-others.

These same percentages seem to hold true for high tolerance for customer contact. Ten percent can't get enough of their customers. Five percent want to be left alone. When it comes to customers, the vast majority can take 'em or leave 'em.

Joy Wright, founder and president of Personnel/Performance Systems, Inc., says, "As a rule, people who are honest like people and they like themselves." In years of pre-employment screening, Joy has discovered that "if somebody is sociable, in most cases they are also higher in character strength and integrity."

Hiring lovers means finding that one person in ten. Here is where the going gets sticky.

First, the likelihood that the boss is a natural lover of customers is also only one in ten.

Second, customer lovers aren't job hoppers. They probably already work for someone else.

Third, with such a shortage of true customer lovers, recruiting and hiring these winners is not enough to be successful. We must discover how to manage that great "situational majority" in such a way that they too will love on the customer.

Ed McGowan is one of the 10-percenters. Not only is he scrupulously honest, he's also a great lover of customers. You should not be surprised.

Of course, there are exceptions to most rules. Still, seeking the 10-percenters will pay off. Not only will they love on your customers, it is also more likely that your money will make it to the bank.

In a little while, we'll give you several dynamite interviewing tips to help you make your final selection. But first you need to know where all those wonderful 10-percenters are hiding.

Birds of a Feather

You heard it first from your mother. When you started hanging out with the notorious Zooberg twins, she shook her finger right under your nose and warned, "Birds of a feather flock together." Hang out with the neighborhood terrorists and before long you, too, would be solidly on the road to Hell.

The principle, luckily, works just as well in reverse. Find one knock-down, drag-out winner and you're hot on the trail of a whole flock of them! Start with your own employees. Which one is a 10-percenter? Next ask her (or him) to help you recruit a friend. Don't worry. They won't just drag in a warm body. Winners like to work with other winners, and that's exactly whom a winner will recommend.

Ask the kid with the "Born to Raise Hell" tattoo to help with recruiting only if you are hiring mercenaries. We have never had an employee quit without notice or attempt to steal cash or merchandise who ran with a crowd of neat, polite friends. It just doesn't happen.

Come and Get Me!

The best way to recruit winners is to let them come to you. They will if you establish a reputation for quality product and service, and for having a great place to work. The losers in life don't expect much of either themselves or others. They will take a job almost anywhere. Why not? They don't expect to stay long anyway!

Winners, on the other hand, have enough self-confidence and self-esteem to be picky about where they work. You want to position your business as a place for winners.

When you promote in the community, you earn, as an important side benefit, top-of-mind positioning as a great place to work. Not everyone will get that message. But the winners you want to attract will read your signal loud and clear.

One of our recent hires is a high school student who received one of our Pays for A's cards that rewarded him with a free drink for each A on his report card. He had been wanting to work, but his parents wanted to wait until the end of the first grading period to be certain that he could handle both school and a part-time job.

When he proudly showed his card to his folks, there he stood with both proof of his performance and an obvious place to look for work.

Hire to the Bench

Stop for just a moment and mentally inventory your crew. Are they all 10-percenters? If the answer, as it most likely will be, is no, then you need to hire.

A full schedule means only that you have covered your shifts. It does not mean you are finished hiring. Your tactic should be to hire to the bench. Assemble a team and then continue to hire until you have a team of all-stars.

Too often, we hire only when there is a vacancy. This results in panic hiring. We body-snatch to fill the position. Then the panic subsides, and we tend to forget that, even though we have a full roster, the team is not up to full strength.

Management must continually be on the lookout for potential winners. When you find one, hire. The worst thing that can happen is that you will have to expand the business to give your winners room to grow.

The problem with winners is that, like cops, they never seem to be around when you need one. If you are serious about hiring winners, you must be prepared to hire one anytime you find one.

When you are served by a winner, pass her a card. Introduce yourself and let her know that you like her style. Better yet, if you have a card or coupon for a free sample from your business, leave one. If she likes you and is interested in your product or service, she

161

will be in. If she isn't happy with her current job, she now knows exactly where to apply.

At the end of especially busy days, we often send someone to a competing restaurant for a change-of-pace snack. This is a little treat for the crew and another way of saying, "Thank you for your hard work." One night it went like this:

"I'd like six chocolate and two vanilla shakes, please."

"Yes, sir!" She smiled, noticing the name of a competing restaurant embroidered on my shirt. "Why are you buying milkshakes?"

"Well, we just set a new store record, everyone is tired, and we sometimes like to take a short break before we start clean-up."

"Your change is $1.87," she announced, before leaning close to whisper, "Do you have any job openings?"

You can't steal happy employees. Unhappy winners are easy picking.

Recognizing Winners

Positively Outrageous Service is playful. It invites the customer to become involved. Involvement on the part of the server requires a high tolerance for customer contact.

In *Service America,* Ron Zemke and Karl Albrecht report that high tolerance for customer contact is essential if the employee is to avoid psychological overload. In simpler terms, it takes an iron constitution to cheerfully handle large numbers of customers, especially when they arrive in rapid-fire order.

Any business will have its share of superstars as well as a number of just-get-bys. What may not be obvious is that traits that would seem to guarantee success in one business may invite failure in another. The same is true of the characteristics required for performing in various levels of the corporate hierarchy.

In the mid-80's, we ran a psychological profile on several hundred unit managers and assistant managers. The theory was that if we could discover psychological similarities between successful managers, then by hiring new manager candidates who matched the profile, we should experience a lower wash-out rate during the training process. Also, these psychologically selected candidates should be expected to achieve mastery earlier and turnover at a lower rate.

That was the theory.

In reality, our profile indicated that, indeed, successful unit managers did exhibit personal traits that were markedly different from those branded as unsuccessful. We determined success or the lack of it by a relatively uncomplicated formula involving sales, unit level profits, and sales increases over the previous year.

So far, we had a program that must have come straight from Heaven, until we looked at the profiles for assistant managers. Much to our surprise, we found that assistant managers in successful stores had decidedly different personality traits than their managers. Too bad. The career path to management included posting as assistant manager!

In short, we found that many of our most successful unit managers had met with considerably less success as assistant managers. We discovered that our most successful unit managers had management styles that almost guaranteed failure at the next level up, multiunit supervision.

According to our survey, assistant managers worked harder and longer than successful unit managers. That was also true for unsuccessful unit managers, who, we discovered, actually worked longer hours than their successful counterparts.

The best managers, it seemed, delegated only sparingly, a trait that would be certain death for multiunit supervisors.

Conclusions: (1) You can't define a winner until you first define the job; (2) a winner is not a winner in every situation; and (3) your "best" employee may not always be your most successful.

In our operation, we have an assistant manager who is prolific at churning out ideas for serving and promoting outrageously. Unfortunately, he doesn't particularly enjoy being the focal point of public attention. Our manager, on the other hand, also contributes to the brainstorming sessions. His ideas are often unusable in their first-offered form, but he, more than any of us, enjoys basking in the limelight.

Fortunately, all 10-percenters do not look and act alike. Loving on customers does not require every employee to plaster on a smile and walk around in polyester leisure suits with white belts and shoes. Positively Outrageous Service can be borderline bizarre, but elegantly engaging service may also qualify as Positively Outrageous Service.

To recognize a 10-percenter, though, does not require a degree in rocket science. You need only one working eye and a few minutes of undivided attention.

In an article on customer service in the *Wall Street Journal,* Dennis Schmidt, assistant vice-president of methods, training, and security for Delta Airlines, was quoted as saying that Delta looks for high-customer-contact tolerance in newly hired flight attendants. I asked him how Delta, clearly a customer service leader, manages to select the 10-percenters. Is it testing? Special assessment centers? What?

According to Schmidt, whom I promised to report as six foot six and good-looking, "There's nothing magic about it."

Oh, yeah? Well, putting together one of America's finest airlines is magic. It just turns out that Delta uses everyday garden-variety magic to do it.

Delta employs flight attendants to screen applicants because, according to Schmidt, "They've been there" and know at least intuitively what it takes to handle tired travelers and squirming babies.

"It's just a kind of sense or a feeling," says Schmidt. "We try to see if they can carry on a dialogue. You have to be able to exchange information to serve the traveling public."

And there lies the first step to hiring a 10-percenter.

The first question in an interview goes to *you:* "Do I feel good while talking with this person?" In a world of first impressions, why not let your first impression be the guide?

Want to be absolutely certain? Then follow this patter exactly.

SCOTT'S NO-FAIL 10-PERCENTER FINDER

"It's not unusual to get really angry at a customer. Everyone does at one time or another. Still, there's a big difference between doing something overt like getting physical with a customer and something like gently putting a rude customer in his place.

"How many times in the last six months have you felt it was

necessary to get tough with a customer? Tell me about the worst incident."

If you want to be certain you are not being conned by someone who pours on the charm just to get past the interview, the above line of questioning will do the job. Here's how it works.

First, you establish a psychological environment that invites the applicant to be "normal" when you say, "It's not unusual to get really angry with a customer. Everyone does at one time or another."

Next, you send a signal that you are aware that there are extremes of behavior and imply, though you never say so, that you sympathize. "There's a big difference between doing something overt like getting physical with a customer and something like gently putting a rude customer in his place."

In the third step, you ask for an example of getting tough with a customer. Because you have stated that such behavior is not unusual—everyone does it—and that you recognize extenuating circumstances, the applicant will feel compelled to at least tell you something.

This is psychologically equivalent to "Do you still beat your wife?" Any admission is an admission of poor customer relations. It will be up to you to decide if, under the circumstances, according to your sense of ethics and customer service standards, the behavior was or was not acceptable.

"How many times in the last six months have you felt it was necessary to get tough with a customer? Tell me about the worst incident."

In this last step, the answer you get will first tell you how often this individual goes into psychological overload. The second question is the most important. The answer that follows will tell you precisely how this person deals with customers.

The 10-percenter, even though your question has made him feel obligated to tell you something, will tell you that in his opinion, getting tough with customers just isn't okay.

Of course, there will be that occasional situation in which the customer was physically threatening, when even the nicest of the nice would resort to self-defense. But since the interviewee will describe the incident, you can evaluate whether his response was appropriate according to your standards.

That 85 percent majority, though, will more than likely give you an occasion or two when "the customer is always right" went right out the window. Here you must listen closely to the situation and then make a determination about this person's service potential.

The bottom five percent will quickly weed themselves out. You don't need any coaxing about how to evaluate "I told the *!?!* to get out and stay out!"

Watch applicants who use terms like "stupid" or "rude" when talking about either customers or fellow employees. These terms tell you that even their best service, while it may be word perfect, will come across as forced.

The point to remember is this: You cannot evaluate information you do not have. Unless you ask an applicant questions that reveal attitudes about customer service, you won't discover the truth until too late. Remember, too, that after you've asked for a description of worst-case customer service incidents, you must ask plenty of follow-up questions. If you mentally fill in the blanks, the only one who is being interviewed is you.

There really isn't any magic to picking the 10-percenters. Like cream, they will rise to the top. In an imperfect world, it may not always be possible to hire only the very best. But a few minutes spent in casual conversation is all it takes to determine whether you are dealing with one of that vast majority who, with proper leadership, can learn to truly love customers.

8

GETTING ORDINARY PEOPLE TO SERVE OUTRAGEOUSLY

CEO Gordon Dames of the San Diego County Credit Union jumped into the car and headed into the evening rush hour traffic. His mission: deliver a replacement credit card to a credit union member who was leaving town in the morning for a two-week vacation.

He needed that credit card.

After hours and way beyond the call of duty, his credit union delivered. And not just the office clerk. Not a branch manager. The president and chief executive officer himself.

Gordon Dames is that kind of guy. He knows when an opportunity to serve outrageously presents itself.

Elsewhere in San Diego, at Farra's Dry Cleaning, customer Carla Johnson arrived to pick up her order. Everything was ready. Everything, that is, except her husband's shirts, which he needed for a business trip.

"I must have had an upset look on my face," says Carla, "knowing my husband was going to need those shirts. I went home with the clothes that were done, and as I walked in the door, the phone was ringing. It was the owner of Farra's. He wanted to know if I was going to be home, because he would finish the shirts himself and deliver them to my house."

Those are two examples of Positively Outrageous Service. Neither customer expected to be rescued from their situation. But thanks to heads-up, service-minded thinking, two disappointed customers have a story to tell.

Notice, please, how those stories change if you leave out the fact that Gordon Dames is president and CEO of his credit union and omit the fact that Mr. Farra himself finished and delivered the shirts.

Some years ago, a survey of restaurant patrons revealed that high on the list of reasons for selecting a restaurant was the amount of status that the staff accorded the guest. Not surprisingly, when it comes to status it seems that no one can bestow status like the boss or the owner.

Among the two, the owner wins hands down in the status race. As Stephen Michaelides said, a customer would rather deal with a dumb owner than a sharp manager. Think about it.

This is not to imply that only owners or managers can be effective outrageous servers. It is to say that in the best of all possible worlds, an owner or manager can be most effective when they are free to personally serve the customer.

But how about ordinary employees? How do you get them to give meaningful Positively Outrageous Service?

- Hire outrageously.
- Model, measure, and reward Positively Outrageous Service.
- Accord the employee personal status through title, freedom of choice, uniform, even ownership.
- Empower the employee to serve outrageously.
- Support outrageous mistakes, and reward outrageous service.

HIRING OUTRAGEOUSLY

This section is not a cop-out. You really can get ordinary people to serve outrageously. But face it: Some folks are indeed determined losers. So why stack the deck against yourself and swim against the tide of a dour personality?

How many people would love on customers like Mike, a manager at McGuffey's Restaurants?

A gentleman rushed out of the restaurant only to run right back in. He had locked his keys in the car and needed to pick up his child from school in a matter of minutes. Mike put the guest first as he calmly handed the man the keys to his new sports car, with the simple instruction to return it when finished!

One of the trainers at Disney, Wendy Snelson, is a vivacious smile of a woman who sparkles her way into a crowd and within seconds is the center of attention. There is something special about her that is visible from fifty feet. It's her smile.

When Disney is hiring, they look for a smile.

A smile confers status.

Status is at the heart of Positively Outrageous Service.

Serving outrageously is another way of saying, "I care."

Employees who don't care won't serve outrageously.

WHY WE HIRE THE WRONG PEOPLE
- Our expectations are too high for what we are willing to pay.
- The position is not clearly defined.
- We hire on emotion, not facts.
- We get in a hurry and make snap decisions.
- We do not consider the manager's personality in relation to the new hire.
- We have not researched our mistakes of the past or held exit interviews.
- We do not have frequent performance reviews or hold meetings to enhance communication.
- We spend more time and money on equipment than we invest in the new employee.

· We wait until the last minute to hire and do not take the time to train.

—Joy Wright, Personnel/Performance Systems, Inc.

Positively Outrageous Service begins with good hiring. In simplest terms, especially for service jobs, there are only four key characteristics that truly matter.

Can Do

Ninety-three percent of all job failures have little or nothing to do with lack of ability. Employees who lack the skills to perform are obvious candidates to pass over. However, lack of ability is rarely the cause of job failure. The problem with Can Do is that it is overemphasized at the expense of the other, much more important traits.

Can Do takes on more importance in technical careers. But even then, it is often not as important as Will Do.

Will Do

If an employee can do the job but for some reason will not do it, all the training and experience in the world is of no value. Typically we say the person is unmotivated. That thinking misses the mark completely.

It is not accurate to say that anyone is unmotivated. The truth is that if they do anything at all, including sleeping on the job, they are motivated. They are just not motivated to do what you want them to do.

The most likely situation is the case of the employee who does only the minimum to keep his job. You've seen this with kids. Mom usually puts out a warning, something like "You're cruisin' for a bruisin'," to let you know that you could get swatted for the next infraction, regardless of its significance.

Too bad we can't do that in the business world. Employees whom we suspect of coasting would be sent to Mom's office. She would scowl and say, "Okay, I've had just about enough. Mind your p's and q's, and don't you dare even look at me crosswise. Do you understand me?"

"Yes, ma'am."

And things would be better.

In the grown-up world with unions and labor laws, employees can coast along at minimum performance seemingly forever. Here is where they call in the "motivational speaker," an absolutely worthless addition to any program unless you are willing to settle for forty-five minutes of humorous anecdotes and have a high tolerance for bubbly aphorisms. If you are the victim of this, be patient. It only lasts a few days anyway. With those who need it the most, it doesn't sink in at all.

No, when you have a Will Do problem, you have a problem in the personnel office. Still, if you are stuck on a team of "coasters," you only have three options: leave, get used to it, or learn how to close the "motivation gap."

Maximum possible performance

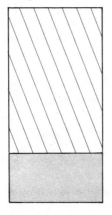

Additional performance acquired by closing motivation gap

Minimum performance required to keep job

Motivation Gap

The Motivation Gap is located just north of the Cumberland Gap. It is quite large and probably responsible for the lion's share of America's poor showing in terms of productivity.

There are two causes for the motivation gap. The obvious cause is that American workers have been presented with insufficient incentive to work closer to their peak performance capability. The less obvious cause of the gap is that American managers have learned to expect miserable performance and are satisfied when they get it.

We were guilty of the very thing when we first opened our restaurant. It never was as clean as it could have been. The service was never as fast and as friendly as possible.

Today, with sales nearly double those of our early years, our restaurant has never been cleaner. The service has never been faster or friendlier. And the product has never been fresher or tastier. On those rare days when sales fall to "preexpectation" levels, our crew is both bored and disappointed.

Higher expectations, I believe, account for the obviously higher standards of operation, a crew that customers constantly comment about as having "high energy," and—surprise! surprise!—record sales volumes. And we aren't finished yet!

The big question remains: How to close the motivation gap once you have your expectations in line? Well, hang in there. That's coming up soon.

Feel Good

The third trait to look for when you are building your team is Feel Good. We've already discussed the point of hiring smilers, people who will extend a personal relationship to your customers. But just how do you know when you have a live one on the line?

Simple. Spend a few minutes in casual conversation. If you wind up feeling good (and you don't have to quantify this scientifically), chances are you've got a winner on your hands. It shouldn't take you long to decide. In fact, if after more than a minute or two you don't have a strong, positive intuitive message, call in the next applicant. After all, most service jobs—and nearly every job is a service job—rely heavily on first impressions.

The nicest customer comment card we ever received included this simple statement: "Employees seem pleased to serve the customer's needs."

That's it!

Fit

Almost three out of four hires are decided largely over the issue of fit. In the best of all possible worlds, almost all hiring decisions would be based on fit. In that case, you would hire with the idea that you already have such a wonderful crew that you want to be careful not to "hire down."

Sony understands the importance of both Feel Good and fit. They use a series of five interviews to screen applicants. They look for high achievers, A or B students with a record of service in school or civic organizations.

What is most interesting is that Sony is less concerned with the content of the answers than with the conversational style and manner of the applicant. You can train a new employee in the technical aspects of the business a lot easier than you can shape Feel Good and fit.

Because businesses are not essentially different from professional sports teams, it makes good sense that every new hire should be evaluated in terms of the potential to hurt or help the performance of the team.

If all business were conducted in a large domed stadium with a national television audience watching, hiring would be much different.

The Monday morning quarterback who analyzes and criticizes every trade by the local professional sports team would get religion when it comes to hiring to fill a vacancy on the sales team. Instead, because the element of competition is not so obvious in the business world, we end up body-snatching and pass off a poor hire as not all that consequential.

"How important really is the guy who helps load trucks at night?"

As the real team players of industry will tell you, he's very darned important.

Good news, sports fans! Just as a shrewd trade can boost the pitching staff of your favorite baseball team and positively impact the old win/lose record, good hires can help improve your own game stats as well. Here is where hiring to fit can be either a brilliant move or a terrible idea.

If you have a great team and are careful not to contaminate it through careless hiring, then hiring to fit makes sense. Beware, though: Every crew has a collective personality. That personality flavors the atmosphere and is immediately perceived by the customer.

It is also perceived by the rest of the team. Make enough poor hiring decisions and not only will you lose customers, your winners will begin to feel out of place and move on to a place where they fit again.

On the other hand, if you are unhappy with your present crew, you can raise the level of the water by hiring not to fit the personality of the team but rather to fit the profile of the ideal. If you find yourself in this position because you inherited a crew of Bart Simpsons, hang on. You can make a difference.

If you are responsible for hiring a team of underachievers, then there is bad news for you: You are the problem. Worse news: People tend to hire in their own image. That rude person over there on the telephone could be you without the suit. Keep it up, pal, and they'll come and take your suit!

MODEL, MEASURE, AND REWARD
POSITIVELY OUTRAGEOUS SERVICE

The most effective way to promote Positively Outrageous Service is to serve outrageously. No matter what theories of training you may have heard, in the final analysis people learn by doing. The most likely behaviors to be "tried on" by new employees are those things they observe on the job. These are the behaviors most likely to be mimicked. These behaviors are most likely to become habits.

And just who is the number-one example? The boss, of course!

If you expect your employees to serve outrageously, you must be personally committed to serving as a visible standard.

We'll talk more about the idea of a visible standard in a later chapter. For now, just keep focused on the fact that you are the model against which employees compare their behavior.

Measuring Positively Outrageous Service

First train them to beat their average. Then train them to beat their best.
        —*Charles A. Coonradt,* The Game of Work

Before you commit yourself to measuring Positively Outrageous Service, examine your motives. If your motive is to punish the laggards, go back to square one. Too often when management, particularly management known for being all stick and no carrot, announces the creation of a feedback system, employees run for the hills. They understand very well, thank you, the subtle difference implied between "evaluation" and "feedback."

Evaluation carries the connotation of "We're going to document just how awful you really are performing." Feedback doesn't come across all that much friendlier, but it leaves more room for praise. And praise—positive feedback—is the point of the exercise.

This is not to imply that poor performance should be hidden. On the contrary, poor performance must be recognized, and recognized with the idea that it is not acceptable and that change for the better is expected. The subtle difference comes from these two facts:

Criticism stops behavior.
Praise encourages behavior.

If the only feedback an employee receives is in the form of criticism, she will quickly develop an absolutely awesome repertoire of behaviors "not to do." She will, however, be left without a strong message about what behavior is desired.

The tough job of enlightened management is to praise poor performers. Poor performance itself should not be the object of praise, but improved performance must be praised. It is the praise that makes continued improvement possible.

175

When we began the practice of weekly inspections at our restaurant with the idea that the manager's bonus base amount would be multiplied by the inspection score, we did not begin by inspecting fairly. We decided consciously to err on the side of our management. Things that today would be absolutely unacceptable were in the early days not noted on the form.

We felt that being brutally honest would indeed be brutal. Such tough measures from the beginning would probably have been so discouraging that progress would have been slow in coming, if at all.

Since we began this practice, weekly scores have improved a little, but the operation of the store and the quality of the crew, their service, and their product have improved, along with sales, tremendously.

Today, if you walk away from one of my picky, picky inspections with a 95 percent, you've done something absolutely wonderful.

The above idea is so important that here it is restated in fewer words, with capital letters:

NEVER LOWER YOUR STANDARDS,
BUT EXPECT MORE EVERY DAY.

Ken Blanchard once told a wonderful story about Shamu the Killer Whale. In academic terms, it is a story about "successive approximations of desired behavior." You'll enjoy it more told in English.

Whales do not normally jump out of the water to cross over ropes suspended above the surface. This rope jumping is not normal whale behavior. But whales can do it if they are taught.

The problem is that whales do not speak English. Just as German shepherds speak German, whales speak, what? Eskimo?

Anyway, whale trainers have to figure some creative way to communicate the idea of rope jumping to killer whales. Now they could install surveillance cameras to watch the aquarium and then come in once a day, check the tape, and, if there was no rope-jumping behavior, beat the whale with a stick. (Why not? Managers do this to people all the time.)

Or the trainers could show a fish to a hungry whale and wait until it jumps over the rope. Then a grateful trainer would rush over and feed the whale. The problem is since rope jumping is not natural whale behavior, and since we've established that whales do not speak English, it's most likely that the whale would either jump at the trainer in an attempt to get the fish or eventually take up swimming on its back more or less permanently.

The best whale trainers teach the trick of rope jumping by suspending the rope midway between the surface and the bottom of the pool. When Shamu swims under the rope, nothing happens. When Shamu swims over the rope, *voilà!* A fish!

Now here is the tricky part. The trainer must begin to raise the rope in small increments. Otherwise, as Blanchard so astutely points out, it would be a pretty stupid whale trick. "Look at that, ladies and germs. There he goes again!"

Like the folks at our restaurant, the whale must constantly improve performance to continue to get a fish. The whale likes fish, but our management is complaining that their freezers are full!

What 'n' How

Whatever you measure and reward you will get.

The behavior you reward is always the behavior you get. People are not stupid. They do things that are rewarded. You usually get stupid behavior when "stupid" is rewarded. And we reward the darndest things. Take the behavior of arriving late for a meeting, for example. People are often rewarded for being late: They don't worry about the traffic; they are the center of attention when they arrive; and, best of all, the meeting starts as soon as they arrive—no waiting!

A young woman entered at the back of the darkened auditorium. She walked quietly up the center aisle, selected a seat in the front row, removed a magazine from her purse, and began to read.

I was setting up equipment under the dim work lights on the stage.

"Excuse me, miss. Do you know we don't start for an hour?"

"Uh-huh."

"I guess you had trouble arranging transportation," I offered.

"Nope."

"Gee, why did you come so early?"

"You don't know me, but I was late to your last seminar. I didn't know you would lock the doors, and I got left out. I didn't want to take a chance on its happening again."

There it is. Reward late, you get late. Reward being on time and—ta-da!—you get on-time behavior.

(I trained almost an entire corporation simply by locking the doors at the posted starting time!)

The problem is making absolutely certain that you are rewarding the behavior you want. For example, you may decide to reward units produced per hour. Without qualifiers, you may end up rewarding the prolific production of junk. Decide to reward new-idea generation and you'll get ideas all right. But what about the quality of the ideas?

Of course, rewarding quality without regard to units of output can kill productivity.

The best incentive systems employ push-pull measurement/rewards. For example, we reward increased sales *and* making the labor budget. That way the need to give improved customer service is counterbalanced by the reward for "making labor."

The System

Incentive systems will help close the motivation gap. The rules for developing a system that works are:

Get input from everyone involved.

Keep it simple.

Expect it to change.

Just as you ask your commercial customers what kinds of products, services, and amenities will motivate them to buy, you must ask your employee customers what will motivate them to work at their peak performance. After all, they "buy" their bonus with their behavior.

You will be pleasantly surprised at the creative, reasonable, and effective ideas your employees will generate. We'll talk more about designing feedback systems in a later chapter.

Keep it simple. Incentive plans must be based on simple, easy-to-use-and-see measurement. Complicated plans are often counterproductive. If an employee cannot clearly see exactly how the reward is determined, the system will be ignored.

When you design your feedback/incentive systems, do so with change in mind. A trial period, not linked in any way to compensation or bonus plans, is suggested. Be certain to try only one program at a time so you can be absolutely certain of cause/effect relationships.

Design measurement systems to be employee-monitored. To be truly effective, create feedback systems that are as near instantaneous as possible. The longer it takes data to translate from behavior to feedback, the less valuable the data. Early data means early correction when performance is below standard.

A close to pure feedback system is at work when you drive your automobile. Turn too far to the left and the bumpety-bump of the dots on the center line tell you to make an immediate correction. Overcorrect and the sound of your hubcap rubbing the curb accompanied by pedestrian screams gives you a hint to make another adjustment!

Feedback, feedback. It tells you how you are doing.

> Officer to hit-and-run victim: Did you get a look at the car?
> Victim: No, but I'm sure it was my mother-in-law. I'd recognize that laugh anywhere.

If immediate feedback has the most value, then it follows that responsibility for effective measurement systems must be placed in the hands of the employee whose behavior is being measured.

TEAM: Together Each Achieves More

The question arises: Reward the individual or the entire team? Yes.

While individual feedback is an absolute necessity for closing the motivation gap, if rewards are given only to the top performer, the system can actually backfire. Let's say you and I are competing for the top sales prize. We are close in points when you notice that I'm doing something that could lose a sale. Are you going to help me? Probably not.

What if we were competing as a team? Now that's a horse of another color. Rewarding team effort has the effect of creating synergism. Let's amend the opening tag to read "Rewarded Together, Each Achieves More."

Another effect of measuring individual behavior and rewarding only the top performer is that poor performers are quickly discouraged. They immediately see that they are outclassed and quit trying. In fact, their efforts may be even less than if there were no feedback at all. Worse, these discouraged employees may even begin to bad-mouth the system, negatively influencing the performance of others.

ONLY OWNERS WILL GIVE
POSITIVELY OUTRAGEOUS SERVICE

We began this chapter by describing the power of status confirmed when the boss is personally involved with serving the customers. The entire basis of effective management is the leveraging of one's time and consequent ability to impact the business through creation of "boss surrogates": employees acting on behalf of and with the delegated authority of the boss.

Vice-presidents have more status than department managers only because they have more of the CEO's delegated authority. One key to getting ordinary people to serve outrageously lies in discovering ways to delegate to them more of the boss's status. This does not necessarily imply that authority must be proportionally delegated, but within limits it helps.

180

Employees can be given status through titles—(everyone at a bank is a vice-president); uniforms; freedom of choice; and, of course, actual ownership.

Every business should at the very least get its employees into an attractive (let them be the judge) uniform. This promotes a sense of team, of belonging, and it clearly communicates to both employee and customer who is in charge.

That is the least you can do. Best is to give everyone a stake in the success of the business, if not actual ownership. And a stake in the business doesn't have to be complicated. A simple bonus paid for breaking hourly, daily, or weekly sales records will do wonders toward sparking employee interest. Just remember to make the goals attainable, and keep in mind that the younger the work force, the shorter the attention span. (More about this in the following chapter.)

EMPOWER THE EMPLOYEE TO SERVE OUTRAGEOUSLY

Empowerment, as we will see, is absolutely necessary if you expect Positively Outrageous Service to occur in your operation. If an employee lacks the authority, chances are slim or none that he will venture out of the box when he spies an opportunity to deliver Positively Outrageous Service.

But beyond the idea of simple authority to act is the value of merely bestowing the power. Holding power is roughly equivalent to being trusted and respected, essential ingredients to a feeling of ownership.

SUPPORT MISTAKES

Support outrageous mistakes. Reward Positively Outrageous Service. The first time an employee runs for the border to deliver Positively Outrageous Service, you can bet she will look both ways to see if she is going to get clobbered. The first attempt at P.O.S. is likely to be a timid step beyond. If that is rewarded or at least goes unpunished, the next attempt might be a little bolder. But the first time an employee gets punished for going too far, the motivation gap will be back to its original "let's don't do anything more than we have to" size.

The first mistake should always be free. It must be accompanied by encouragement to try again.

Be prepared to be surprised.

At the Corning Company, the employees have been organized into some 3,000 teams of up to fifteen members each. The result: Profits are up 250 percent since 1982.

Eastman Kodak essentially turned over management of its professional film manufacturing unit to the folks on the factory floor. In 1989, the unit came in $1.5 million under budget, a $2.5 million improvement!

PROOF OF THE PUDDING

Linda Cooper is head of First Chicago Bank's consumer affairs department, a job she likens to "running a business emergency room." Her job is to solve problems, to keep customers from waiting too long, to straighten out tangled accounts and damaged relationships.

A normal manager would keep track of things, hold "smile" seminars, and distribute happy-face buttons. Lucky for First Chicago Bank employees and customers, Linda Cooper is abnormal. She shapes behavior.

Cooper knew that she couldn't effectively change behavior without first defining clear, measurable goals: Exactly how does the customer perceive First Chicago Bank? How can we know when we are improving?

Cooper and her crew discovered approximately 200 quality indicators. This is especially remarkable because few businesses measure more than one or two, if any at all. Cooper's goal was then and remains today to "measure, measure, measure."

Listed below are twenty-five of Cooper's quality indicators of customer service, just to get you started thinking about your own operation.

TWENTY-FIVE SERVICE ATTRIBUTES RANKED
IN ORDER OF IMPORTANCE TO CUSTOMERS

1. Being called back when promised.
2. Receiving an explanation of how a problem happened.
3. Providing me with information so I know what number(s) to call.
4. Being contacted promptly when a problem is resolved.
5. Ability to talk to someone in authority.
6. Being told how long it will take to solve a problem.
7. Being given useful alternatives if a problem can't be solved.
8. Being treated as though I am a person, not an account number.
9. Being told about ways to prevent a problem in the future.
10. Being given progress reports if a problem can't be solved immediately.
11. Ability to talk to the service representative without interruption.
12. Not being put on hold without asking me.
13. Being treated with appreciation for my business.
14. Having an actual person answer my call rather than a recording.
15. Being told the service representative's name and telephone number.
16. Getting through to the customer service department on the first call.
17. Being offered suggestions on how to keep my costs of banking services down.
18. Ability to speak with someone on the first call who has the authority to solve a problem.
19. Receiving an apology when an error is made.
20. Being helped without being put on hold.
21. Having the phone answered by the third ring.
22. Being greeted with "Hello" or "Good morning."
23. Ability to reach the service area after 4:00 P.M.

24. Being addressed by my name.
25. Ability to reach the service area before 8:30 A.M.

Linda Cooper set out to empower an organization that in three short years grew from three facilities to sixty-five, a growth rate that would be difficult for most organizations to even survive. With help from Cooper, First Chicago Bank has done more than survive; it has handled its growth with something akin to grace. Certainly there were rough spots, but not nearly what might have been expected.

"Empowerment is difficult," says Cooper. "You can't empower if the form is stupid or the copier doesn't work." With that in mind, Cooper established her department as a problem-solving organization that works as well for employees as it does for customers. In fact, it's fair to say that Cooper's department of consumer affairs works for customers precisely because it works for employees.

Such support inspires employees and creates the sense of ownership that might be expected in an organization that listens.

To attack service problems directly, Cooper has created a number of incentive and recognition programs. What is most important to learn from her is the decision to reward outstanding performance with shares of First Chicago Bank stock. What better way to promote ownership?

To challenge branch employees, the Customer Service Olympics were created. If ever there was an idea worth stealing, this is it. In the Customer Service Olympics, mystery shoppers called branches at random with a typical problem. The branch was evaluated by three standards:

- Could they answer the question?
- Could they solve the problem in a single referral?
- Did the overall tone encourage the mystery shopper to answer yes to the question "Would I want to bank here?"

A coded list of standings was delivered to each branch, along with a verbatim transcript of the mystery shopper phone calls. To make the Olympics even more meaningful, selected competitors were also shopped.

The real question is "Does it work?" You be the judge. Linda Cooper's "Supreme Court of Service" fixes 75 percent of customer complaints within twenty-four hours. More important are the problems that do not occur because of First Chicago Bank's commitment to fix problems before they have a chance to reoccur.

Empowerment, measurement, and incentive—concepts powerful enough to close the motivation gap. Powerful enough to get ordinary people to deliver extraordinary service—Positively Outrageous Service.

SERIOUS ABOUT SERVICE

"The behavior you get is indeed the behavior you reward." American Express executives must have that phrase tattooed someplace prominent because nobody seems to reward Positively Outrageous Service quite like American Express. If you are serious about serving outrageously, then show it.

"Great Performers" is the American Express program designed to reward unexpected, out-of-proportion, highly personal acts of service.

Does it work? Read and marvel at the following excerpted letter from co-chairmen Edwin M. Cooperman and G. Richard Thoman.

> Dear Colleague:
>
> In 1990, travel-related service employees helped customers stranded in Nepal, Trinidad and the Philippines during government uprisings, evacuated more than one hundred Westinghouse employees from Saudi Arabia, and assisted clients involved in a plane crash in Honduras. In these and scores of less dramatic instances, employees truly went above and beyond the call of duty in an exemplary way to help their customers.
>
> One hundred and sixty Great Performers were selected worldwide in 1990. Sixty-nine of these regional winners have been chosen Grand Award winners, an increase of 35 percent over the previous year.
>
> Last year a new award level—the Great Performers Hall of Fame—was created to honor employees who have won the Grand Award more than once. Five employees will be inducted into the Hall of Fame this year, bringing the number of employees who have achieved Hall of Fame status to 10.

In addition, 32 employees received a Special Award for their service in the aftermath of the San Francisco earthquake.

We are proud of our involvement in the Great Performers program and look forward to another year of Great Performances!

Great Performers receive cash awards of up to $1,000 as well as the recognition and admiration of their thousands of peers worldwide. The Grand Award winners are even more richly rewarded. These employees receive an all-expenses-paid trip to New York for two and $5,000 in American Express Travelers Cheques just for starters!

The results speak for themselves. . . .

Adel Zakaria Assaad. When two customers arrived for a tour in Cairo, they discovered their travel agency had declared bankruptcy and their tour operator had not been paid. The tour was leaving early Sunday morning, not enough time to get the required funds. Adel gave one woman 200 Egyptian pounds of his own money. When $4,000 in cash was wired from her husband to the travel service office, Adel took a six-hour bus ride to bring the money to her. He then took a 1:00 A.M. bus back to Cairo.

Max Belin, Cathy de Gannes-Martin, Carol Patino. When eighteen missionaries from Omaha, Nebraska, were stranded in Trinidad during an attempted coup, Max, Cathy, and Carol worked together for four days to evacuate the group, overcoming bad phone connections and local curfews to get needed medical attention, arrange for charter and commercial air transportation, meet and assist in Grenada, and provide complimentary hotel accommodations and meals.

Gregory A. Botkin. On Valentine's Day 1990, a Card member called from Illinois to report that he had ordered special roses to be delivered to his wife and they hadn't arrived. Greg called the vendor, who couldn't deliver them until two days later. Greg called many florists and finally located the roses; but the store wouldn't hold them or accept the card over the phone, so he purchased the roses in person with his own card and personally delivered them to the Card member's wife.

Kelly Foote. Kelly helped a stroke victim (who was in critical condition) by arranging to have him transported from the island of

186

St. Kitts to Miami. He contacted the doctors at their homes for special permission for the victim to pay the bill when he returned home. Kelly also made sure the hotel would cash the travelers checks from the patient's companion even though they were signed by the patient; Kelly referred his companion to the Special Handling Unit in order to get an approval for a $9,000 charge on her corporate card to pay for the air ambulance. In a matter of hours, the victim was receiving treatment in a Miami hospital.

Joseph Level. A man was killed while vacationing in the Cayman Islands and his seriously injured wife was flown to the United States. The deceased man's sister called Amex and asked Joseph if the unused portion of the round-trip fare could be used to transport her brother's body home. Joseph called Northwest Airlines and was told that the deceased was no longer considered a passenger but cargo instead. The body was still in the custody of the Cayman Island authorities and was at a funeral home on the island. Joseph found it is not common practice to embalm a body in the Cayman Islands, so he arranged for an embalmer to fly from Miami. The funeral home agreed to perform all necessary services to ensure the body's return to the United States. Joseph also discovered that flight insurance entitled the deceased's estate to $150,000. He then arranged for Northwest Funeral Service to fly the body to Washington, D.C., to be picked up by a local funeral service. He also suggested that the funeral home become a service establishment—they agreed.

Vito Patrissi. Vito went to deliver train and airline tickets to a client's home. Unbeknownst to him, the client had moved and hadn't updated his profile. The next morning, Vito went to the Hartford train station prior to the 6:30 A.M. departure and held a sign with the client's name on it. He met the client and gave him the tickets.

Trish Shephard, Michael Taylor. On December 28, 1989, a severe earthquake hit Newcastle, N.S.W., killing fourteen people. The city was closed for one month, millions of dollars' worth of property was destroyed, and all communication with Sydney was down. Within one hour of the earthquake, Trish and Michael departed with

$20,000 in Australian cash, $20,000 in U.S. travelers checks, and a mobile phone. They established an Amex location at a rep office. Throughout the next four days, Trish and Michael operated a twenty-four-hour service, helping many customers.

Don't Leave Home Without It!

9

MANAGING OUTRAGEOUSLY

The first responsibility of a leader is to define reality; the last is to say "thank you." In between, the leader is a servant.
—*Max DePree,* Leadership Is an Art

While working as a supervisor at a Louisiana chemical plant, Kevin Coxon was startled to hear his name mentioned on a local radio station. Did he really hear that he had just won the daily "Best Boss" contest? It seemed so unlikely that he was hesitant to call the station to claim his prizes. After all, to win you must be nominated by your employees.

Kevin knew he had been working hard to win the trust of his crew, but "Best Boss"? No way. Previous management had had such serious problems dealing with the all-union work force that the thought of "Best Boss" seemed remote, if not impossible.

Kevin's tactic had been simple: honest, open communications at every opportunity. With a little coaxing, he managed to get most of the group to form a softball team, sponsored at Kevin's request by a major contractor to the plant.

At the urging of a co-worker, Kevin called the station, and indeed he was a winner. But the prizes weren't what excited Kevin.

"The best part was that these guys, who were supposedly at odds with management, would do that for me. My boss was shocked. 'It's not supposed to be that way.' "

Now, years later, Kevin smiles and says, "I've still got that plaque."

Beyond assembling a team of winners, employees with the skill and personality to serve, management has only three simple responsibilities:

1. Clearly define the task at hand.
2. Remove obstacles and provide tools.
3. Say thank you for a job well done.

In other words: Management supplies the Go-Power.

GO-POWER!

G   Goal
O   Objectives

P   People
O   Ownership
W   Work design
E   Example
R   Reward

Goals! If you don't know where you are going, how will you know when you get there?

Positively Outrageous Service focuses on product and service. Outrageous management does the same. And therein lies the problem. Ask employees to tell you the mission statement of their company and you are likely to get no more reply than a blank stare. Ask how they personally relate to that mission statement and you risk inducing a coma.

Once a manager has recruited a new member to the team, the first task at hand is to clearly define the mission. *Everything* that follows should relate to the mission. Anything that doesn't contribute to accomplishing the mission is worse than wasted effort. It is actually counterproductive, because time and resources were spent that could have otherwise have been put toward the mission.

A mission is forever. Goals are for the year or perhaps as long as five years. Objectives are the small, measurable steps that are milestones on the way to our goals.

No company does a better job of defining goals and motivating their employees to reach them than In-N-Out Burgers in southern California. Here is a company with higher unit volumes than McDonald's and an almost nonexistent marketing program. There isn't a better example of a company that has stayed true to its vision, focused on Four-Walls Marketing, than In-N-Out Burgers.

Their concept is perfect for a chain that is national in scope. "Fresh, high-quality food and fast, friendly service" could be the motto of a thousand restaurant chains. The difference is that at In-N-Out Burgers, quality is more than a slogan, it's a way of life. In-N-Out Burgers has grown slowly and remained a regional favorite, so that they could keep their eye on the details that make the difference. At In-N-Out, employment starts when a clear vision is effectively communicated to even the newest, lobby-sweeping, hamburger-flipping employee.

PURPOSE/MISSION STATEMENT
(PRIORITIZED)

In-N-Out Burgers exists for the purpose of:

1. Providing the freshest, highest-quality foods and services for a profit, and a spotless, sparkling environment wherein the customer is our most important asset.
2. Providing a team-oriented atmosphere whereby goal setting and communications exist, and providing excellent training and development for all of our associates.
3. Assisting all communities in our marketplace to become stronger, safer, and better places to live.

It was an American Airlines flight from Dallas to Maui. The good folks at Continental Bondware had hired me to speak at a gathering of In-N-Out Burgers's top-performing managers and their spouses. In-N-Out managers who had met their goals—and that was almost all of them—were being treated and feasted for a solid week at the beautiful Maui Hilton.

When the flight attendant passed by to offer drinks, I jokingly requested a vanilla shake.

"Sorry," she said. "Fresh out of vanilla shakes! But if you look straight down, we're flying over California and the best vanilla shakes anywhere."

"You must be talking about In-N-Out Burgers," said a gentleman seated across the aisle.

"You bet I am, and I could go for one of their burgers about now, too. Why don't I ask the pilot to send you out for lunch!"

There's something about a company that stays focused on product and service. You don't have to be at 33,000 feet to find out what it is.

POWER TO THE PEOPLE

> *We take eagles and teach them to fly in formation.*
> —*Wayne Calloway, CEO, Pepsico*

Flying in formation, that's the goal. But notice just what or who is flying in formation. Eagles, not turkeys.

There's a rather disgusting bumper sticker that reads, "It's hard to soar with eagles when you work with turkeys." What's wrong with this picture? It's an admission that management is not doing its job. On the face of it, you might think that the employees, the "turkeys," are being slammed. But think a little deeper. Just who is responsible for hiring? The employees? Of course not! If you don't like the employees, the buck stops at the top!

Turned-on organizations start with turned-on leadership that defines the goals, sets the course, and then goes on a crusade to recruit a battalion of like-minded followers. For every hero of Positively Outrageous Service, there is an unseen hero of empowering leadership.

Donna Paproski of the Mile High Kennel Club has a daughter who works in a hotel. Perhaps the daughter gets her sense of hospitality from Mom, but even a natural tendency isn't likely to blossom without support.

Here's an example. The hotel was totally full when an entire basketball team showed up. The team had traveled all day only to discover that not only was there no room at the inn, there were no other available rooms nearby. In an act that would make a mother proud, daughter Paproski sent the team to the dining room for dinner, sent the bellman out for rental cots, and converted a conference room into an impromptu but comfortable barracks. All this at no charge.

Outrageous? Of course! And I bet you'd like to steal an employee! Well, I'd like to meet the manager who would empower an employee to serve so outrageously!

Possession Is Nine-tenths of the Law

My idea is almost always better—because it's mine. Smart managers promote ownership. They know that even a second-rate idea enthusiastically implemented beats a stroke of genius acted out haphazardly. And assuming that employees have second-rate ideas misses the truth by a mile.

The truth is that employees have terrific ideas. The problem is getting them to express those ideas. Here are three solutions:

1. Remove the risk from thinking creatively.
2. Reward problem solving.
3. Make ownership the easiest alternative.

Humans learn at an early age to stay within the comfortable confines of conventional thinking. Too often conventional thinking is no thinking at all.

Raise your hand in school and offer a far-out idea or solution and all too often the response is anything from rolled eyes to "You've got to be kidding!" Too few teachers and, later in life, managers have the poise and sensitivity to say, "That's an interesting idea! How did you come to think of the problem like that?"

Managers should, within reason, make well-intentioned failures risk-free. The first mistake should be a freebie. Death by deep frying is still an acceptable response, but only for a repeat mistake.

"I notice that you spent $53.48 to have the plastic light cover replaced."

"It cost a little more than I expected."

"I had a similar reaction. Three dollars and forty-eight cents was about what I had in mind. The $53.48 was a real surprise. How did it happen?"

"Well, we couldn't find one at the hardware store that would fit, and since we didn't have the tools to cut one to size, and since we knew it had a priority with you, we called the electrician to see if they had one."

"Looks like they had a pretty good one!"

"They said they could cut a cover and drop it off on the way to another job. And, before you knew it, they had installed it and left us a bill, and I didn't know what else to do."

"Do you know how to handle it next time?" I said with a tight, very forced smile.

"If it happens again, I'll die before we spend that much money!"

"Exactly what I was thinking."

Reward problem solving, not buck passing. When passing the buck is rewarded over solving the problem, almost inevitably the root problem is that the company has lost sight of its original mission. The Nordstrom's employee mentioned earlier had the proper perspective when he said, "We are trained to make the customer, not the sale. We are trained to make customers."

Sales made, forms completed, and phone calls answered are all very effective ways to measure activity. They are lousy ways to measure the level of service. Too often pay plans are constructed in such a way that these deceptive measures of service effectiveness are recorded and rewarded.

If, for example, Marriott rewarded its telephone operators only for answering the most telephone calls per shift, this story would never have been told:

Jim Conlan of M & M/Mars arrived later than he wished at the Denver Marriott. Jim described himself as tired and grumpy, a condition quickly remedied by quick, pleasant "no problem" responses to his requests for a nonsmoking room close to the elevator, a $200 check cashed, and help with his car, luggage, and dinner reservations. Each request, says Jim, was greeted with a smile that said, "I'm happy to take care of you."

"Following a good dinner with good service, I asked the Marriott operator for recommendations for a hotel in Dillon (where there is no Marriott). Within minutes, the operator called back with a list of hotels, complete with their phone numbers and addresses."

If Albertson's Supermarkets rewarded employees only for cash in the till, you wouldn't have heard this story from Rick Vincent of United Artists Theatres in Denver:

"While shopping at Albertson's Grocery one evening, I was having difficulty locating an item. Finally I gave up and took my purchases to the register. The checkout clerk asked me if there was anything else I needed. When I commented that there was something I couldn't find, she left the register and brought it back!"

Problem solving is also rewarded when you defer to employee opinions: "Let me ask Tom to handle that for you. He's our expert in that area." Not only does this give Tom pride of craft, it lets Tom know that he has greater-than-expected latitude in his area of expertise.

The best way to reward problem solving is to make problem ownership easy, or at least easier than problem passing. Here are three suggestions:

1. Provide a range of solutions.
2. Refuse complaints unaccompanied by solutions.
3. Refuse to accept ownership.

When the only tool you have is a hammer, you tend to treat every problem as a nail. Give your employees more tools, and teach them how to use them.

My grandmother likes McDonald's sausage and biscuits. She also likes pickles. Too bad because, try as she may, Gran can't get Mickey D's to part with a pickle. Pickles aren't supposed to go on sausage biscuits.

So imagine my elderly grandmother walking into McDonald's ordering a sausage biscuit and then carefully adding a single slice of pickle that she brought from home. Got any idea why "Have it your way" is *not* the slogan of the Golden Arches?

If you forget to pack your own pickle, here's a suggestion: Order a hamburger and ask that they leave off the mustard, ketchup, meat, and bun. *Voilà!* You'll have the pickles you need!

Or you might want to look for someone trained and empowered by Robert Farrell, founder of Farrell's Ice Cream Parlours. Jim Hayes of CARE Co. relays this story:

A new waitress didn't know quite how to respond to a long-term customer who ordered an extra pickle with her sandwich.

"You can order a side of pickles for a quarter" was the response.

"I don't want a side order of pickles. I only want one."

"Well, I can sell you a pickle for a nickel."

With that the customer picked up her purse and left, probably forever. When Farrell received a letter from his unhappy former patron, he was furious. For the price of a lousy pickle, he was losing a valuable customer.

When Farrell says, "Give 'em a pickle," he means that too often we lose valuable customers over insignificant issues.

Hey, Mickey D's! Give 'em a pickle!

It's probably closer to the truth to say that most McDonald's are owned by quality- and service-minded individuals. And you'd have no problem at all getting a pickle, even a handful of them. What is important is that even if it's your policy to "give 'em a pickle," it's of no consequence if your employees aren't aware of their options. It's fine to have a "give 'em a pickle" policy. But it counts only if you shout it from the rooftops!

Managers keep employee thinking to a minimum when they listen to complaints without demanding that each be accompanied by a solution. Turn chronic, unproductive, spirit-killing complaining into positive action with this simple line: "That's interesting. What are you willing to do to help solve the problem?"

Passing the buck is a skill picked up in childhood. How many "Family Affair" comics have you seen where one of the kids suggests that "nobody" spilled the milk, broke the glass, or tracked in mud?

They say that old habits are hard to break. But this one is an exception if you'll just remember to use these magic words.

"Hmmm! That's interesting. How are you going to handle this?" These magic words are all you need to keep ownership from passing from an employee to you. Bill Oncken, a great teacher and thinker, specialized in the science of Monkey Management. Bill thought of monkeys as "anything that requires you to make a decision or take action." To Bill's way of thinking, monkeys belong almost exclusively to employees.

"It's the manager's job to help employees with their problems," he said at a San Antonio seminar. "And how can you help someone without a problem? Therefore," and here follows a long, pregnant pause, "it's the manager's duty to be the sole source of his employee's problems!"

He meant it!

Employees too often want to give their problems—their monkeys—to the boss. "What should I do?" or "I don't know how to handle this one" are, through the eyes of Oncken, smoke screens through which the aware can spot a monkey leaping from an employee's back and landing in a pile on the manager's desk.

"There is nothing so beautiful as the sight of an employee leaving your office with a monkey firmly screwed to his back! Because then you can help them!"

The best way to keep those monkeys from becoming airborne is to use these simple words that, as a cross wards off vampires, keep monkeys securely at bay. You simply say, "Hmmm! That's interesting. How are you going to handle this?"

Send Your Employees to P.E.

Work design. That's an abbreviated way to refer to the physical, procedural, and authoritative characteristics of an individual job. The most essential work design element for turned-on, empowered employees is P.E.—Project Empowerment. Nothing motivates like results. Unfortunately, too few employees ever see the fruit of their labor. Too few employees are given whole tasks, tasks that have a beginning, middle, and visible, measurable resolution. This is also true of problem solving.

Some years ago, a major insurance company hired a consultant to "motivate" its vast army of claims processors. It seems that the rate of claims processing had fallen frightfully low, a problem the company had attempted to solve by adding more bodies to the sea of desks that already occupied acres of headquarters office space.

After careful study, the consultant made a simple, no-cost recommendation: Deliver mail in the morning, and pick up mail at shift's end.

The recommendation makes more sense when you think about the rest of the job design. Each desk had a large in-basket and an equally large out-basket. Claims came in and were processed, then dropped into the out-basket. Every hour or so, a mailroom clerk would pick up processed claims and deposit another load of fresh claims.

Since most of the claims processors were women, the old adage "A man works from sun to sun, a woman's work is never done" seemed doubly appropriate. It exactly described the problem: The processors were totally demoralized because they never seemed to be making any progress. Just about the time their in-basket reached empty, a mail clerk would come by and fill it again. That was bad. Worse, though, was the fact that the out-basket was emptied at the same time. In other words, the employees never had a chance to see the results of their labor.

With mail pickup limited to the end of the shift, the workers could enjoy a sense of accomplishment.

Every job should have something that employees can count or otherwise measure as a symbol of tasks completed.

Feedback delayed is feedback denied. Equally as important as having something that can be physically measured as a sign of achievement is the idea that employees should be able to measure for themselves.

Ken Blanchard uses the analogy of bowling with a sheet covering the pins. You roll the ball, it runs straight and true, it slips under the sheet, and a tremendous clatter is heard. Then your boss peeks under the sheet and says, "You got two."

"Two? Hold up that sheet and we'll both count!"

There is the story of Frito-Lay putting counters on their bagging machines so that the operators could have a visual record of their performance. Simply adding the counters and requiring the operators to make entries in a production log dramatically increased productivity.

These examples of the relationship of feedback to physical productivity also illustrate the importance of feedback to the more emotional issues surrounding problem solving for customers.

Deny me the opportunity and responsibility of seeing a problem handled all the way to resolution and you may as well not ask me to help at all. Even if I help a little, it will still be difficult to muster personal, emotional energy. After all, it really isn't my problem.

Look at the difference between the valet and the manager in this next tale. Which one had the responsibility and authority to handle the entire problem? And who got the Feel Good of setting things right?

Dan Gallery, of Carts of Colorado, arrived at the Hyatt Chicago O'Hare after a long day made even longer by a delayed flight and heavy traffic. The valet did not have a pen and asked to borrow one from Dan. Dan's new Cross pen had special meaning because it was a gift from his wife to celebrate his company's election to the *Inc.* 500.

Later, when Dan reached for his pen, he discovered that it was missing, most likely still with the valet. He called the concierge, who, rather than handling the problem, suggested that he inquire at the valet desk. She said she doubted that the valet had lost his pen. The pen remained missing.

A furious Dan Gallery fired off a hot letter to the hotel's general manager. When Dan returned to the office, there on his desk was a letter of apology, a new Cross pen, and an offer of three free nights' accommodations, plus fruit basket, wine, and complimentary room service!

Of course, we have to give that Hyatt general manager great credit for his customer-saving, out-of-proportion response. Losing a pen is unexpected. Losing a special pen can be highly involving. It took extraordinary service response to both salvage and increase customer affinity.

But you have to wonder how the story would be changed if either the valet or the concierge had been to P.E. If they had Project Empowerment, the responsibility and authority to handle a problem in its entirety, how much better could Dan's story have been?

It may not be realistic to give valets the authority to order up Cross pens, complimentary lodging, and free room service. Or is it? How would the story play out if, instead of a hotel, Dan had lost his pen at Nordstrom's?

HAND-TO-CHIN

"Hand-to-chin" is an entry in my seminar notes. It's a cue for me to act crazy and involve my audience in a quick game of semi–Simon Says. At the end of the game, I'm usually standing on a chair or table facing a sea of laughing faces when I yell, "Grab your chin! Grab your chin!"

Of course, I grab my cheek.

And so does nearly everyone else.

Not my cheek—theirs!

Why? Because when it's all said and done, when theory runs into reality, people learn by doing. Not by listening. Not by reading. People learn by doing.

Monkey see, monkey do. The behaviors that people are most likely to try are those behaviors that they see in their environment and can imitate. If you don't see it, you are not likely to try it. If you don't try it, you won't learn it.

And so, for all our fancy training programs, sophisticated lesson plans, handbooks, and flipcharts, in the end our everyday operations are our most effective training program. Like it or not.

Whenever you interact with your environment, you have a learning experience, whether or not you are aware of it. Each interaction is followed by a consequence that may seem important but could just as easily be missed as insignificant.

Paul Mudloff of the United Artists Theatre Circuit recalls a childhood experience:

"I attended a theater when I was a young boy at a summer matinee. It was the first time I attended the theater, and the place was packed. We all waited for the show to start, and when it was time, the theater manager (owner) walked down to the front of the theater with his staff and introduced his staff to 600 screaming kids.

"After the introductions, he invited 600 kids to sing 'God Bless America' with him, after which he promised we could all scream as loud as we wanted . . . until the movie started.

"It not only provided good feeling and a good time but also made me want to work for this man as well as attend movie events at his theater."

Did you notice Paul's career choice? You just never know when the example you set will have a lasting, significant impression.

We hired a young man against all better judgment and put him to work in our restaurant. This was years before our volume grew to the point where we could somewhat hide a less productive employee. At lower volumes, everyone has direct customer contact. Still, I was confident that in spite of his awkward communication and social skills, we could teach him to give at least passable customer service.

In our place, everyone can hear both sides of the conversation at the drive-through, because the customer's voice is broadcast via speaker. The drive-through becomes an ideal place to serve as an example, since everyone hears your service patter as well as the customer's response. When I'm at the store, I head straight for that position so that I have a chance to reinforce the customer service example. "Playful" is a good description of my approach to service at the drive-through. Interacting via a metal speaker can seem downright impersonal unless the server takes extra care to sound friendly and approachable.

After a few mornings listening to my example, our awkward new employee volunteered to take a shot at the drive-through, clearly the most demanding position in the store. I reminded him that suggestion selling is important to good customer service. I told him to relax, have fun, and be sure to always offer a drink, perhaps by saying, "How about an ice-cold soda to wash that down?" How was I to know that his very first order would be to a thirsty construction worker who only wanted something cold to drink?

> Employee: Good morning! May I serve you?
> Customer: Give me a large cola.
> Employee: Would you like some hot, battered french fries to wash that down?

The customer was so surprised that he ordered the fries, and our beaming employee was so encouraged that he managed to sell a two-piece chicken dinner "to round that out."

Excellent customer service occurs only when employees have an excellent, visible standard that they can imitate and against which they can compare their own behavior. The good news is that the standard is always visible. The bad news is that the visible standard is not always a *visible standard of excellence.*

As the owner, CEO, or manager, you bear the special responsibility of being the most visible standard. If you are in any way unsatisfied with your employee's customer service behavior, there is only one first step to take. Look in the mirror!

CARRIES A CHAINSAW BUT GETS GOOD RESULTS

The behavior you get is the behavior you reward. In times of high unemployment you can get away with chainsaw management. But the instant people decide that they can find a better job elsewhere, they start to bail out in droves.

An old-time manager just smiled when I proposed an incentive program to help stem the tide of massive turnover. "Incentive?" he said. "We give 'em an incentive every day. Do your job and you get to keep it."

Interesting concept, but worthless in the 90's.

A manager is the keeper of the rewards. She can reward behavior with a smile, a verbal or written acknowledgment, sometimes a prize or monetary reward. Management looks like this:

Step one: Hire capable members to the team.

Step two: Define the mission.

Step three: Arrange for the tools and time necessary to achieve the mission.

Step four: Use rewards to focus behavior on the mission.

We're on step four. Step four is the most difficult. Some managers rarely think to reward mission-focused behavior. They remember to punish undesirable behavior while completely ignoring the importance of rewarding good performance.

The problem with this approach is that criticism and other forms of punishment (negative rewards) serve only to *stop* undesirable behavior. They do absolutely nothing to *start* desirable behavior.

Praise and other positive forms of rewarding behavior move the organization ever closer to the mission. Negative rewards may halt backsliding, but they do nothing to cause a move forward.

Managers who hide the carrot and carry a big stick kill any chance of creative customer handling. After all, who wants to chance getting clobbered if something doesn't work out perfectly or fit policy exactly?

That's not to say that, when things go wrong, managers should ignore poor performance. It is to say that, even when you do criticize, you should not strip away an employee's dignity.

One of the nicest stories ever took place at the end of the day at Durrin's Dry Cleaner's in Kerrville, Texas. Owner Chet Whatley called his crew to the back of the store one evening right after closing.

"I'm sorry for all the yelling I've done around here lately. And I'm sorry for all the yelling I have left to do. But I do appreciate all the good things that maybe I forgot to mention."

With that, he presented each employee with a single red rose.

After all these years, "thank you" remains a powerful motivator, especially when delivered sincerely and publicly. But there should also be some tangible rewards for those who serve with pizzazz.

You don't think saying thank you has that much value? Well, take this!

A survey by Dr. Roger Flax, president of Motivational Systems, asked this question: If another company with a reputation for giving recognition and praise offered you a similar job with the same salary and benefits, would you quit your current job?

Now quitting a job is a pretty stressful act, so making a change just for better recognition is a major decision. Still, more than a fourth (27 percent) of all workers surveyed said they would leave. Nearly two out of three (67 percent of those who said they would quit their jobs) work for companies where recognition is rarely or ever given.

A *USA Today* survey discovered that 44 percent of those currently employed expected to hold the same job for the next three years. Fifty-six percent did not.

Recognition, reward, is a powerful tool. If you are not good at it, get good at it. Your employees are watching. And so are your competitors!

YOU'RE OUT'A HERE!

Everybody deserves to know every day if they have won or lost.

—Charles A. Coonradt

The secretary who barely had the strength to file her nails is suddenly energized as five o'clock approaches. The warehouse clerk that you couldn't get out of the break room with a blast of dynamite discovers new energy once he reaches the parking lot.

What is wrong with these people? Are they lazy?

These are the people that keep motivational speakers on the road. "Come talk to my people. They aren't motivated."

Baloney!

Everyone is motivated. They just aren't necessarily motivated to do what you want them to do. And why should they be? Work too often just isn't any fun.

When work ceases to be fun, we accuse people of being *un*-motivated. Nonsense! It is that the work is *un*-fun.

When Work Is Play, Employees Are Motivated

Charles Coonradt has made some interesting comparisons between work and play. People are usually champing at the bit to hit the time clock so they can go play. So what is it about play that turns people on? How can we make work more like play? Well, in kids' games:

- The rules and goals are agreed upon at the beginning.
- Players know the score at all times.
- Keeping score makes the game interesting.
- The rules are never changed mid-game.

And I'd like to add these two:

- You get to play with kids you like.
- You play games you are good at.

Compare the rules for kids' games with the reasons cited when people leave their job.

40 percent: Unhappy with management
20 percent: Terminated
20 percent: Do not like the job

How many times in all of the above separations do you expect the word "unfair" was used?

People are criticized or fired because they failed to reach goals they were not aware of or never trained and equipped to achieve. Too often the first time an employee is told the score is the day a raise or promotion is denied or a pink slip is placed in the pay envelope.

Executives are the most likely group to be victims of changed rules. "They created an incentive plan, we worked our tails off to make it work, and they changed the plan when all of a sudden we started making too much money!"

"Didn't like the job" is often another way of saying, "I never knew where I stood" or "I didn't like the people I worked with." If work was a game and you didn't enjoy being with the other kids or they changed the rules just as you were winning, you would take your ball and go home. When given a chance to play for another team, that's what we all do. It's just that adults call it a "career change."

Poor morale leads to employee turnover. Most of the nine top reasons cited by Personnel/Performance Systems, Inc., look like close relatives of the rules for kids' games.

TOP CAUSES OF POOR EMPLOYEE MORALE

1. Undesirable work environment
2. Improper materials or equipment
3. Lack of feedback
4. Inadequate benefits
5. Insufficient pay
6. Poor management, lack of training
7. No orientation, sales, or product training
8. Inconvenient parking
9. No organized approach or vision to direct efforts

Here's a summary of the above: I don't know what we are doing, and if I did, I don't know how or why or with what we would do it. And if I did, the rewards wouldn't be worth the effort.

TEN THINGS TO TRY

1. Hire to Fit

Southwest Airlines has improved hiring by creating recruitment ads that more accurately reflect the personality of the company. Because Southwest Airlines bills itself as a fun airline, complete with Fun Fares and peanuts, sometimes called Luv Bites, it made sense to have a recruitment ad featuring head honcho Herb Kelleher in an Elvis outfit and captioned with the headline, "Work in a Place Where Elvis Has Been Spotted!"

This from the same airline that surprised and delighted passengers and onlookers with a mondo-bizarro parade to draw attention to the airline's new digs at the Phoenix Sky Harbor Airport.

Stepping out of the baggage-claim area, I was bowled over to first hear, then see, a huge marching band playing "Joy to the World," followed by the Sun City Poms, a group of geriatric but still very much alive body-suited seniors. Bringing up the rear was a battalion of Southwest employees in various stages of formal attire—top hat, tails, and short shorts was a typical outfit in this very untypical outfit.

Southwest has figured out that a stuffed shirt might look great in one of their parades but definitely would not fit the employee profile.

A unique hiring technique helps insure that new employees will fit the customer as well as the staff. Southwest frequent flyers, called Company Club members, are invited to assist in the prehire screening process. The theory, and it seems to be a good one, is that customers will know best what qualities will make for a successful Southwest flight attendant.

2. Improve Benefits

You don't always get what you pay for. You often get less, and you seldom get more. Au Bon Pain, a northeastern chain of sandwich shops, pays nearly twice the industry average, on the premise that if you want the cream of the crop, you are going to have to pay for it.

The payoff has been in decidedly lower turnover and a staff that approaches what some would call fast-food work with a refreshingly professional attitude.

When it comes to pay and benefits, you don't have to be far above average to still be above average. All other factors being equal, improved benefits may be a significant edge in the bid for a quality work force.

3. Formal Mission Statements

Just what is it that makes your operation special, different, better? If you don't tell your employees, how can they act out the careful words of the business plan?

Every employee deserves to know exactly what is expected of him or her. A formal orientation program is nice, but it's not the only approach that works. Perhaps simply requiring management to team up directly with your new employees for their first few hours on the job will be sufficient.

A written mission statement, like the one we saw from In-N-Out Burgers, is a must. Post it. Live it. Keep it visible.

4. Train, Train, Train

Stress is often cited as a major factor in employee turnover. "Stress? You've got to be kidding! I do all the thinking!"

Sure you do. All the thinking and none of the explaining. The how and why of every operation may be clear as day to you, but it's clear as mud to a brand-new employee. You wouldn't believe the number of employees who say, "I never could figure out exactly what they wanted me to do." They usually say that on their way out the door.

5. Evaluate, Evaluate—Dance to the Music!

Employee evaluations are ways of helping the employee keep score. They should be frequent, objective, and never directly linked to compensation.

Too often we witness an employee "oops" and respond with a "memo to file." Why tell the file? The file doesn't care! It gets depressed holding all those negative memos! Tell the employee!

Every day is evaluation day. Get *The One Minute Manager* and learn from a master how to give praise on a *daily* basis. Save written evaluations for less frequent but more in-depth discussions. Just remember, like verbal feedback, written feedback should stick to the facts. Give me the facts, ma'am—the *measurable* facts.

Don't you dare evaluate attitude! You are not buying attitude. You are buying behavior!

6. Reward Service Excellence

The words "above and beyond" are often used when people tell me their tales of Positively Outrageous Service. Company-sponsored service award programs cannot match the value of hiring naturally nice people—the 10-percenters. But they do offer encouragement and help spotlight custom service–minded behavior.

Making an example of excellent service gives permission to the uncommitted majority. It also gives them an avenue for the recognition and praise that we know people crave.

Cindy Cesnalis is the director of service strategy for La Quinta Motor Inns. She has direct responsibility for showcasing customer service excellence. When a La Quinta employee is nominated for a Customer Service Excellence Award, Cindy and staff wrestle with the tough decision of who will receive the monthly award for the most extraordinary service incident. La Quinta stories would fill a book. Here are just a few favorites.

Extraordinary Service Incident: Diana Martinez, Eagle Pass, Texas. Diana helped a National Guardsman who was a guest at her property. The Guardsman got word that his wife was having difficulty while giving birth; he asked for and received leave to return home. However, it was close to midnight, and the next scheduled bus would not depart for fourteen hours. Diana immediately loaned the distressed soldier her own automobile so that he could leave at once. The Guardsman returned her car, with a gift, three days later.

Extraordinary Service Incident: The Entire Staff, Fresno, California. On the morning of April 14, 1989, an elderly guest who was with a tour group from England was rushed to the hospital by ambulance. Mr. Gibson had suffered a massive heart attack and was given a 50-50 chance of pulling through. The tour bus pulled out of Fresno, leaving Mrs. Gibson alone in a foreign country. Mr. Gibson was released from the hospital on April 26, but the doctor would not allow him to travel until May 8. Mrs. Gibson writes, "I will never ever forget any of you. You kept my courage up, filled me with such love for you, each and every one."

The employees reached out to Mr. and Mrs. Gibson. While Mr. Gibson was in the hospital, they escorted Mrs. Gibson to the hospital and arranged for the staff there to look after her. They made long-distance calls for Mrs. Gibson and brought food to her room. On several occasions, they picked up groceries for her and took her to get groceries. They even gave Mrs. Gibson a birthday party. The staff dropped by her room continually to see if she needed anything. The front desk staff loaned Mr. and Mrs. Gibson the inn's refrigerator for the remainder of their stay.

The next one is so wonderful, we'll let the customer tell the story.

Extraordinary Service Incident: Bernard Adams, Schaumburg, Illinois.

Dear Manager:

On 19 October, I phoned your Inn to ask about having a rose secured for my wife, who was a guest at your facility then. I have had a practice of giving her some type of flower or plant every Friday for the last twenty-five years and was eager to see what could be worked out on that particular Friday.

Mr. Bernard Adams answered your phone. When I asked him what was possible to do about ordering a single rose, he informed me that, although there was no florist at the Inn, he would find a rose for me and deliver it to her room. I was most pleased at the professional and polite manner in which he responded.

When I asked him about how he would be able to do that, he said that there were street corner vendors nearby and he would see to it that she got a rose. I told him he could charge it to the account or that I could send him funds. He quickly replied that it would not be necessary to do either. He would care for the matter personally—it would be his way of extending a courtesy in the name of positive customer relations.

I travel extensively and know what a hassle you and your people have with some guests and the unusual requests they make. Mr. Adams was polite, helpful, and professional. Later that evening, I got a call from a surprised and pleased spouse, who had received the rose via Mr. Adams.

To say that I am pleased with the quality of your service would be a gross understatement. Try delighted, ecstatic, euphoric.

Mr. Adams took his time to assist a stranger with a strange request and did it with professionalism and class. As a senior supervisor myself, I recognize quality when I experience it. Mr. Bernard Adams is a quality worker. You are fortunate to have him with you. I appreciate what he did but, more than that, who he is and how he responds to people. Those are qualities that cannot be "hired" at any price. A person either has and shares those qualities or does not. He has them and uses them effectively in representing your organization.

Please express my appreciation to Mr. Adams. I will also express my appreciation to your national office. People are all too quick to "beef" when things go wrong. I believe in being just as quick when quality service is delivered. Commendations are in order.

Thank you for caring.

R. C. Steneakken
Chaplain (Colonel), U.S. Army Staff Chaplain
Fort Richardson, Alaska 99505

These are stories you expect to hear with a name like Marriott or Hyatt attached. But, in fact, Positively Outrageous Service can be found in your operation. Think of creative ways to recognize your most caring employees.

La Quinta flies their monthly award recipients to the headquarters city of San Antonio. A Cadillac is rented for the lucky guests, who then become the center of attention at the corporate offices. Of course, they are also treated to a grand tour of San Antonio and its attractions. But I think the most memorable part must certainly be the recognition.

How do *you* recognize your service superstars?

One way not to do it is to have an Employee of the Month award that is merely a matter of whose turn is it this month. An employee recognition program that is not meaningful is actually counterproductive. Establish measurable standards and offer a reward that is truly motivating to your employees. What kind of award is that? Ask them! They'll be glad to tell you!

The stories from La Quinta were so nice, I couldn't resist a callback to Mike Nosil, vice-president of the human resources department and Cindy Cesnalis's supervisor. I wanted to know why Cindy's title was director of customer service strategy.

According to Mike, " 'Strategy' creates in the mind the idea that we are internally committed, versus just something that is done externally. We wanted to set up something more than a bitch and complaint department. Market share can't be manufactured. You must steal it—or earn it—away from the competition." La Quinta's service team is doing just that.

7. Focus, Focus

Speaking of asking your employees, employee focus groups are one of the best ways to generate ownership and creative marketing ideas as well as reduce both theft and turnover. Whew! That's a lot to achieve from such a small idea!

Employee focus groups give everyday employees an opportunity to have a say in how their jobs are structured. Surprisingly, these groups, properly guided, will more than likely generate policies and procedures nearly identical to those handed down from the Zecutives at the Puzzle Palace. The difference? Employee ideas will be better because they are *their* ideas.

The same is true for employee marketing ideas, with one small twist. Employee ideas for marketing and promotion will come with fewer of the "that's too different to try" labels attached. True, the ideas may need to be tempered by the realities of budget and perhaps law, but employee promotion ideas will almost always be the most fun. The most creative public relations firms are often staffed with young people who don't have the "good sense" to know why their harebrained ideas won't work.

Reduced theft as a result of employee focus groups seems at first like we're stretching the point. But it's a fact. People don't steal from themselves. Focus groups create so much ownership that employees don't want to ruin "their operation" by stealing from it.

A good way to tell how badly you need employee focus groups is to listen to employees describe your product, service, or prices. If they speak in terms of "our product, our service, our price," good for you. If you hear "their product, their service, their price," you're in big trouble.

> Customer: How does this air conditioning maintenance plan work?
> Employee: Well, you pay the company a monthly fee. If you have any problems, you call them and they'll come out and fix it.

Compare the above with:

> Customer: How does this air conditioning maintenance plan work?
> Employee: We charge a small monthly fee that usually works out to be less than what you would expect to spend on an annual basis. We come out and perform a twenty-point maintenance checklist twice each year. If you have any problems at all, just give us a call and we'll be right out!

Employee focus groups lower turnover because employee complaints are not allowed to fester unresolved. Employee complaints lead to employee solutions. Don't like the way things are going? Well, don't blame management. You set the policy!

Employee focus groups have the added benefit of building team strength. Employees learn that they are both capable and expected to solve problems—together.

8. Theory of Relativity

Turnover will decrease—or, more positively, retention will improve—almost the instant management compensation is linked to employee retention. Managers pay attention to the darndest things, especially when it affects their paycheck! Pay a monthly or quarterly bonus for employee retention and managers will soon catch the "I love my employees" religion.

They will listen to their employees. They will think twice before instituting new policies. And employees will respond to this nurturing, understanding environment and lose all interest in changing jobs.

213

9. Praise by the Minute

How often did we say you should evaluate employees? How about constantly?

Employees should at least be eligible for instantaneous praise. That's not to say that you have to go around dispensing honey-dripping words constantly, just that you should be prepared to serve a small dose of thanks at the drop of a hat.

How small? How about a real pat on the back as you lean in close and say, "Nice job!" Lean close but not too close. Private praise is nice but not nearly as valuable as public praise.

Public, on-the-spot praise becomes an important part of the training of both the praised and the "public." I behave; you give instant feedback. I have no doubt about what must be done to get more praise!

Just as importantly, the co-worker standing nearby also has a learning experience. "I saw what you did. I saw how the boss reacted. I understand now exactly what I need to do to get some of that for myself."

10. Catch! Take My Keys, Please

My dad always said that you could tell how good a manager really is if he would just have the good grace to break his leg on the way in the back door. As the ambulance attendants are loading him on board the meatwagon, he should be able to toss his keys to the first employee to arrive and sail off to the hospital completely confident that the business would open perfectly and run flawlessly without his attention.

Can you afford to break your leg?

If the answer is no, you have some recruiting and training to do.

The secret is to allow employees to manage themselves when you are there. The benefit will be that they can at least hold down the fort when you are not.

Self-management does not mean that you should put the inmates in charge of the loony bin. Self-management comes from the gradual withdrawal of management support and decision making.

You should have a very specific plan of everyday training designed to turn more and more control over to your team.

You will be absolutely amazed at how much responsibility the average employee can handle when you give her the support and trust she needs, when you release responsibility and authority on a gradient instead of dumping it all on her at once.

Break a leg!

Positively Outrageous Service will never permeate the entire organization until you create and implement a plan for turning over the organization itself to the employees.

If yours is a culture of management by rules and regulations, you shouldn't expect more than a few isolated instances of Positively Outrageous Service. These will happen purely because of the force of character of your 10-percenters.

Establishing a culture that supports Positively Outrageous Service requires management that is willing to play just out of bounds. After all, Positively Outrageous Service is itself out of the ordinary. It is unreasonable to expect an organization that is run by "that's the way it has always been done" management to suddenly give stand-out service. That would be positively outrageous.

It takes stand-out management to build a team and give it the power necessary for Positively Outrageous Service.

10

THE P.O.S. MANAGER'S TOOLBOX

Every human resources professional worthy of a paycheck eventually faces up to the task of predicting human behavior. And why not? The dollars and effort and even heartache invested in hiring and attempting to train new employees who wash out of the program before they earn their first productive dollar amount to a staggering drain on corporate resources.

The cost to companies that practice body-snatch hiring techniques and sink-or-swim training must be even greater, although infinitely more difficult to calculate.

When it was my turn in the box, I turned to Joy Wright, now president of PSI in Bedford, Texas. Joy is a master at predicting the success rate of new hires. If you don't know Ms. Wright, or someone like her, you should. Otherwise you are wasting big dollars on turnover that could be spent on more effective training or—here's a novel concept—dollars that could fall to the bottom line.

A famous marketer once said, "Only 15 percent of my marketing works. The problem is, I don't know which 15 percent!"

Have you ever hired a new employee with the expectation that he would fail? Of course not! (Suspicion, maybe, but expectation, never!) Your problem, like the marketer's, is that while you know not every new hire will work out, you don't know which will and which will not.

Don't get the wrong idea. Even practiced social scientists like Ms. Wright and crew cannot predict success or failure with absolute certainty. What they can do is give you very accurate measurements of character traits that are important to success in any particular job. They can develop a profile of successful candidates against which you can compare potential new hires. The closer the match, the greater the likelihood of success.

Oh, sure, there will be the odd individual who profiles well but insists on crashing and burning. And there will be the applicant given a whole forest of red flags who slips through the system, gets hired, and succeeds in spite of himself. But those exceptions are rare. The rule is that once you have identified the character traits of successful individuals, the closer the new hire matches that profile, the greater are the chances for success.

It's important to note that there is no such thing as a "generic" profile of the perfect new hire. Success is always defined in terms of the job. Would you really expect someone who matches the profile of a successful night club bouncer to match the profile of a successful yoga instructor? Of course not!

If you haven't developed a profile for successful entry-level employees for your organization or at least given it some serious thought, you'd better get to it. If demographers are right, by the turn of the century there will be a tremendous shortage of labor in the United States. Success will belong to those who are able to out-hire, out-train, and out-retain the competition.

To help you with your project, I asked Ms. Wright to develop a profile of someone likely to have a high tolerance for customer contact. If you don't at least start by hiring people who crave customer contact, your chances of providing good service are slim and of ever achieving Positively Outrageous Service absolutely none.

POSITIVELY OUTRAGEOUS SERVICE PREDICTOR

Can you provide outrageous service?

1. I am proud of my accomplishments at work.
2. I have a great deal of confidence in my abilities.
3. I am my own best friend.
4. I enjoy projects that call for rapid action.
5. I typically do well in pressure situations.
6. I enjoy jobs that permit movement and freedom.
7. I enjoy being surprised.
8. I enjoy entertaining guests.
9. I find it easy to make new friends.
10. I have a desire to be someone who is well known and successful.
11. I would enjoy being famous.
12. People think of me as an energetic person.
13. Assuming the responsibilities of a "leader" feels comfortable to me.
14. Many of my close friends have a unique or nonconventional lifestyle.

If you responded "true" to ten or more of these statements, you are confident and creative, and chances are that you like people—all ingredients of outrageous talent.

If you responded "true" to between six and nine statements, chances are that you experience enthusiasm on a more inconsistent basis. At times you can be better than most, and at other times you will be very reserved.

Five or fewer "true" responses indicate a more reserved person who may stick to the tried and true and who requires a great deal of security and conformity in his or her life. Chances are that providing Positively Outrageous Service is not your cup of tea.

POSITIVELY OUTRAGEOUS SERVICE MANAGEMENT QUIZ AND ANALYSIS

Positively Outrageous Service begins with hiring the right individual in the first place. We said it before: The first job of management is to assemble a team of winners. But notice, please, that the bulk of this book is devoted to managing that team.

Try your luck at the Positively Outrageous Service Management Quiz, on the following page, and find out just how well prepared you and your company are to deliver Positively Outrageous Service.

Analysis

Statement #1: When corporate executives regularly take part in serving the customer, they are doing more than simply helping to cement a relationship with the folks who pay the bills. The less obvious benefit is that by personally serving customers, executives who are the "visible standard" communicate that serving others is honorable and that customer service is the focus of corporate energy.

Statement #2: Highly visible feedback systems communicate to the customer not only that she can be heard but also that the company actively solicits customer input. To be effective, feedback systems must get data immediately into the hands of the involved employees so that the mental connection between behavior and consequence can be made. It is equally important to respond to the customer. Such a response rewards the customer for taking time to give input and says in no uncertain terms that the company cares.

Statement #3: Ken Blanchard talks about "legendary service." Legends are stories told over and over about brave and wonderful deeds. It is in the telling of stories that heroes are made. Telling service stories turns ordinary clerks into heroes. Building heroes encourages future service excellence.

Statement #4: Getting it right technically almost doesn't count if the customer also receives a poor perception of commitment to a continued relationship. Training that focuses solely on the technical,

219

POSITIVELY OUTRAGEOUS SERVICE MANAGEMENT QUIZ

Rate your agreement with the following statements. Give each a rating of 1 to 10.

_____ 1. Executives in your organization personally and regularly serve customers.

_____ 2. You have a highly visible customer feedback system that gives immediate feedback to both employees and customers.

_____ 3. Stories about outstanding customer service are regular features of company communications and meetings.

_____ 4. Training in your company gives service training equal importance with technical and procedural training.

_____ 5. Employees from entry level up are highly empowered to make service decisions.

_____ 6. Though mass marketing may be an element of the marketing strategy, event selling and other person-to-person tactics are frequently employed.

_____ 7. Failure is relevant. If you are not failing at least occasionally, you probably aren't growing. First mistakes are free.

_____ 8. Compensation is, and should be, directly linked to contribution.

_____ 9. Change is regarded as important and the "contrarian viewpoint" of challenging tradition is considered praiseworthy rather than dangerous.

_____ 10. When you are a customer, you "play" with clerks, attendants, waitpersons, etc.

_____ Total

procedural aspects of the business is only half done.

Statement #5: It is of little value to talk service unless employees are also empowered to deliver Positively Outrageous Service and rewarded for it.

Statement #6: Mass marketing techniques take on added significance when they are supplemented by event marketing. Event marketing can be done on a grand scale, or it may be only a one-on-one opportunity to deliver Positively Outrageous Service.

Statement #7: Positively Outrageous Service involves an element of risk. After all, P.O.S. Marketing and Positively Outrageous Service are definitely outside the norm. Managers who are punished for straying beyond "That's the way it has always been done" are not likely to try new, possibly dynamite ideas.

Statement #8: Companies in which innovation is not rewarded, in which longevity without contribution is prized, are not likely to make any moves that would make them either outstanding or simply stand out.

Statement #9: Success in the 90's requires at least some internal friction. As long as those holding on to traditions of quality and service allow at least some freedom to marketing contrarians, corporate values will not be lost; rather, they will evolve and survive.

Statement #10: This may be the single most important indicator of your personal tendency to Positively Outrageous Service. The most capable practitioners of Positively Outrageous Service are constantly inviting others to play. "Play" is another word for involvement. It is the company that involves the customer in every way, that creates solid relationships, that will thrive in the 90's.

If your score was 80 or higher, you are probably already marketing and serving outrageously. A score of 60 or higher puts you in the category of "interested but not yet ready to buy." A score below 60 points puts your company on the endangered-species list!

TEN COMMANDMENTS FOR MANAGERS

There's no claim here that the following ten commandments should be carved in stone. But they work for me and they may just work for you.

My list of ten is posted for all to read, and each of my managers has a personal copy. They are not necessarily listed in any particular order. Just like the biblical ten, break any one and I'll personally send you at least as far as manager's purgatory.

1. Be a product, service, and cleanliness fanatic. The operating word is "awareness."

Notice, please, that the commandment has two parts. It's fairly obvious, or at least it should be, that product, service, and cleanliness are the three critical elements of of our business. But I'm not saying "be interested" in product, service, and cleanliness. I suggest that anything less than fanaticism is a halfhearted attitude.

Debbie Fields, founder of Mrs. Fields' Cookies, is quoted as having said, "Good enough seldom is." Think about it.

Part two of this first commandment is "awareness." Your mission is to help your employees see opportunities for improvement. One way is to regularly inspect your operation. For maximum impact, make your inspections unannounced. And here's the big one: Tie bonuses to the inspection score.

My managers receive a weekly, graded inspection. Score 80 percent and you get only 80 percent of your sales bonus. Score 80 percent very often and you get outplacement counseling.

2. Do not say, "I don't know." Say, "I'll find out."

"I don't know" ranks right up there with "It's not my job." As a manager, your job is to develop a team that is so good that the operation runs without you. My team swears that things actually improve when I leave.

People don't "get better," and they don't grow when they are allowed to sit on their ignorance. It's okay not to know; it's not okay not to find out.

3. Do not say, "I can't." Say, "I'll learn."

You can't grow strong leadership by allowing weakness. Adopt the attitude that your people can do anything. Expect them to do it, and then stand by to be surprised at just how resourceful and intelligent they prove to be.

"I can't" just doesn't work with me. Ask me for training and you'll get training. Tell me you "can't" and I'll look for someone who either can or is at least willing to learn.

4. Always try to say "yes" to a customer. Say "no" when it's for their own good.

Two short stories will illustrate.

Our restaurant is in a small town. For some strange reason, a large majority of our guests pay by personal check. When we opened, we didn't accept checks. After all, we reasoned, if you don't have $4 or $5 cash for lunch, maybe you shouldn't be eating out! We turned away a lot of business.

Finally someone put it to me like this: "If I promised to eat at your place once a week all year long, would you be willing to give me a 10 percent discount?"

"Sure," I said.

"If you accepted checks, how many would you expect to bounce?"

"I don't know. Maybe 1 or 2 percent."

"Instead of the 10 percent discount, can I just pay by check?"

Point made. We accept dozens of checks each week. One or two bounce but are quickly collected with a single phone call. Annually we actually lose maybe $100 to bad checks. But just look at all those additional sales!

Story number two:

Last week a car salesman phoned in a delivery order. He asked for a cup of ice and was refused. "I'm sorry, sir. Our boss doesn't allow us to deliver fountain drinks because the ice will melt. Guess that applies to cups of ice as well."

I hit the roof!

I called, apologized, and simply requested that when he call for future orders, he identify himself as "the ice man from Hillstar Motors." For six cents' worth of paper and ice, we have a twice-per-week customer. Saying yes to customers is saying yes to business.

As a side benefit, our out-of-the-ordinary service has brought us even more business from the auto dealership. Twice each month, they order lunch for the entire staff. We deliver tea in gallon jugs and drop off a cooler of ice. The general manager returns the cooler on his way home.

Say no to drugs, but look for creative ways to say yes to customers.

5. Do not ask what to do. Decide and then do it. At worst, make several recommendations, then act.

It's impossible to build a strong team if you make all the decisions for them. Let them make a free mistake now and then if it won't be too costly. Mistakes don't really build character, but confidence and competence that arise from decision making do.

Besides, the way I figure it, if I have to make all the decisions, why do I need you?

6. Ask, "Is what I am doing now improving our product, sales, service, or property?"

There are thousands of things to be done in a business. Most of them count, but some do not.

This is especially true when it comes to promotions and community service projects. Since it's impossible to be involved in everything or to donate to every cause, we always ask one simple question: "How does this sell product?" If the answer is, "It doesn't," we pass. There are too many things that count to waste resources on those that do not.

This is also true for remodeling ideas, staffing ideas, and wild-eyed ideas for new products and services.

7. Be a list master. When asked, "What's on your list today?" always be prepared to show your list.

All of my lead people are required to carry a small pocket notebook. I carry one as well.

Having a list shows you are at least thinking about the business. A list is the beginning of a plan. Without a plan, the business runs you instead of the other way around.

Employees should always have a longer list than the boss's. If not, it's because:

A. The boss does most of the work, which is stupid, because if I'm working, how can I be thinking?

B. The boss does not trust the employees to competently handle important projects. This is a sure sign of poor hiring and training and should cause one more project to be added to the list: Replace the boss.

8. Write every idea and promise on your list.

Ideas not recorded are ideas destined to be lost. Judith Briles, a successful author, says that writing a book seems to clear her mind for more new ideas. Record your ideas as they strike, and be prepared to be amazed at how many more will pop into your mind.

Here's an idea to add to your list right now: Buy a miniature tape recorder and carry it with you always. Ideas that strike while you are driving, waiting in line, or otherwise occupied won't be lost (and often turn out to be your very best).

9. Keep all agreements completely.

If you intend to keep an agreement, write it down so you don't forget. If you do not intend to keep an agreement, don't make it.

Recording your ideas allows them to mellow instead of evaporate.

The difference between the successful and the also-rans is not so much in the quality of their ideas. Successful people implement more ideas. They have more failures, too. But, in a competitive world, a "big shot is nothing more than a little shot who kept on shooting."

10. Manage (think) first; labor second.

The value of a manager lies in leadership, training, and decision making. Manual labor is part of everyone's job, but a restaurant manager washing dishes has no more value than a dishwasher washing dishes.

My managers are expected to be working managers, not nicely dressed dining room fixtures. Both my wife and I take that same hands-on approach when we are in the restaurant. In fact, one of our newest employees commented that he had never seen owners so willing to be physically involved. That isn't necessarily a compliment.

Leaders should always position themselves where they have the greatest customer contact and impact on service. A boss who runs to the office to do something that could be easily handled by a junior employee, or that could be postponed, may be helping. He may also be hiding. Send someone else to the office and stay with the action, where your decision making, training, and leadership can have the most impact.

CONCEPT SUMMARIES

Positively Outrageous Service

- Random and unexpected.
- Out of proportion to the circumstances.
- Invites the customer to play or be otherwise highly involved.
- Creates customer loyalty.
- Creates compelling word of mouth.

P.O.S. Marketing

Defined: Highly involving, perhaps entertaining, event selling done at or near the point of sale in such a way that your product or service develops a unique personality.

Goal: Increase sales by establishing a personal relationship with your customers through point of sale marketing and Positively Outrageous Service.

Characteristics: P.O.S. Marketing is by its very nature:
- Different.
- Low-budget.
- Personal.

Tactics: P.O.S. Marketing requires you to:
- Have fun.
- Get potential customers to your store.
- Get potential customers involved with the product.
- Do something good for others.

PRINCIPLES OF PROMOTION

- Be creative.
- Self-promote.
- Involve the community.
- Focus on product quality, not price.

Anyone can give away product. It takes brains to sell it!
—Unknown

POOR SERVICE? IT'S PROBABLY *YOUR* FAULT!

TEN TIPS TO SUPER SERVICE

- *Be playful.*

  Clerks and waitstaff are often overworked and poorly treated by the public. Customers who attack the store with playful charm are usually received with delight and rewarded by attentive service.

  Gentleman in lingerie store: "Okay, sportsfans. What do you have that's low cut, sexy and in my size!"

- *Tip in advance.*

  To Insure Prompt Service—Sometimes service personnel need a gentle reminder that a tip is optional.

  To parking attendant: "Thanks for keeping my pride and joy. Here's a first installment." (Hand over half of what could be a generous tip.)

- *Award status.*

  Providing service is an honorable endeavor. Take a moment to recognize an individual's contribution.

  To a secretary: "Mr. Jackson is out? No problem! I know who really runs this office. I'm sure you can help me!"

- *Assume.*

  Assume you will get exactly what you want. True, there are some not-so-happy folks handling the public and they tend to assert their power by telling customers that they are out of product or can't change the rules. They are simple to handle. "I understand you normally sell these as a set but I only want one and am willing to pay for it. So do whatever you have to do to make that happen and I'll be on my way."

  or

  "No problem. I don't mind waiting right here while you check with your supplier!"

- *Use humor.*

  Use humor to ask for exactly what you want. Why is it that the

228

same people who treat clerks like simpletons are offended to discover that clerks are not psychic? Use humor. Ask for *exactly* what you want.

"Can you help me find a shirt with 36" sleeves? I seem to have inherited gorilla arms and standard 34/35's just won't fit!"

· *Know when to settle for less than perfect.*

When a store is overcrowded or understaffed, don't compound the problem by attempting to bend reality. Recognize that the employees are busy and chances are, you will get better service than anyone!

"Looks like you folks are getting clobbered. Let me tell you exactly what I need so you won't have to make a second trip."

· *Help yourself.*

When attentive service looks to be totally out of the question, help yourself. It's faster and less frustrating than trying to attract attention. Often helping yourself is a gentle way of getting the attention you deserve.

Never hesitate to: Pour yourself more coffee, commandeer a luggage cart or check the unopened stock for the item you need.

· *Never yell. Go straight to the top.*

Too often clerks do not have the authority to make the decision you seek. Yelling only alienates a potential ally. Your tactic: Ask who can make the decision and go directly to that person.

"Who has the authority to help *us?*"

· *Never blame; just get it right.*

If the order is incorrect or otherwise not satisfactory, never blame the clerk. After all, the clerk can help you set things straight. Always leave open the possibility that you are at fault.

"I'm sorry. I thought I had reserved a full-size car. Can you straighten me out? Thanks!"

COROLLARIES

- Get someone else to pay for your promo.
- Reward everyone if possible.
- Allow vicarious participation.
- Have specific, measurable goals.

WOWING THE CUSTOMER

- Remember the customer even when he is not buying.
- Support causes the customer holds important.
- Give something free of cost and occasion.
- Become a product and service fanatic.
- Entertain the customer (especially while she is waiting).
- Demonstrate that the customer is first by respecting his time.
- Say you are sorry for the slightest slip from standard.
- Ask for the customer's opinion.
- Promote internally.
- Know the customer by name.
- Invite the customer to play.

OPPORTUNITIES FOR POSITIVELY OUTRAGEOUS SERVICE

1. Customers can be selected at random for special—outrageous—treatment.
2. Potential customers can be selected at random for special —outrageous—treatment.
3. Special events can be created specifically for loving on your customers.
4. Customer complaints or comments can serve as cues for Positively Outrageous Service.
5. While customers are waiting, serve them outrageously.
6. After the sale is the perfect time to serve outrageously.
7. Watch for serendipitous cues as triggers for outrageous service.

230

CUSTOMER FEEDBACK SYSTEMS

- Immediate
- Top level
- Sensitive/action
- Extend offer

P.O.S. RULES FOR APOLOGY

- When in doubt, apologize.
- Apologize even when the customer doesn't know you goofed.
- Always make amends in excess of the slip-up.
- Empower everyone to solve problems.
- Handle mistakes by the numbers.

LINE THEORY

- Lines are self-limiting.
- Lines can form only when customers arrive faster than they are served.
- Lines, once formed, persist indefinitely.
- Once service is delayed for any reason, every subsequent customer will wait for the length of the original delay.
- Lines are only as long as they appear.

SCOTT'S NO-FAIL 10-PERCENT FINDER

"It's not unusual to get really angry at a customer. Everyone does at one time or another. Still, there's a big difference between doing something overt like getting physical with a customer and something like gently putting a rude customer in his place.

"How many times in the last six months have you felt it was necessary to get tough with a customer? Tell me about the worst incident."

MANAGEMENT'S BIG FOUR

1. Assemble a team of winners.
2. Clearly define the task at hand.
3. Remove obstacles and provide tools.
4. Say thank you for a job well done.

In other words: Management supplies the Go-Power.

GO POWER

G   Goal
O   Objectives

P   People
O   Ownership
W   Work design
E   Example
R   Reward

PRINCIPLES FOR MAKING WORK FUN (WHY KIDS' GAMES ARE FUN)*

- The rules and goals are agreed upon at the beginning.
- Players know the score at all times.
- Keeping score makes the game interesting.
- The rules are never changed mid-game.
- You get to play with kids you like.
- You play games you are good at.

TOP CAUSES OF POOR EMPLOYEE MORALE

1. Undesirable work environment.
2. Improper materials or equipment.
3. Lack of feedback.
4. Inadequate benefits.

*Adapted from *The Game of Work*, by Charles A. Coonradt.

5. Insufficient pay.
6. Poor management, lack of training.
7. No orientation or sales or product training.
8. Inconvenient parking.
9. No organized approach or vision to direct efforts.

OUTRAGEOUS

Service is a special joy
Not just a job to do.
At least that's the way it's meant to be
So say those folks with Woo.

Loving on customers can be a chore
Or a privilege—it depends
On who's the server, who's the guest,
And the messages we send.

The best kind of service ever given
Is random, unexpected.
If you're kind of crazy, you're just right.
In fact, you've been elected.

P.O.S. is the kind of thing
That once started gets contagious.
And that's the part that makes work fun
When service gets outrageous!

THE BEGINNING

The phone rang. It was the publisher. She had just received chapter 10 of this book.

"I got your last chapter. The book is looking really super, but do you think you want to end such a fun book with a chapter of lists?"

"You don't like chapter 10?"

"Chapter 10 is fine, but why not leave your readers with a really wonderful story about Positively Outrageous Service?"

Positively Outrageous Service was not much more than an idea in November 1990. I had experienced great success with a seminar simply titled "Outrageous Service" and had been encouraged by audiences everywhere to put those ideas into a book. It was the thought of writing that book that got me out of bed in time to attend what turned out to be a life-changing seminar at a National Speakers Association Writers Conference.

At 7:00 A.M. on Sunday morning, most sane people are either in bed or enjoying the newspaper over breakfast. Writers apparently aren't all that sane. I joined several dozen kindred spirits in a seriously overcrowded room to hear Viki King present a seminar that either was or should have been titled "Writing the Book That Is Inside You."

Viki King is an earth-woman. She has a Debra Winger voice: half whiskey and the rest the sound of low-to-the-ground nature. You can easily visualize her driving a 1962 Volkswagen van with daisies and peace symbols painted on the windows. Yet she lives in Malibu and has written for some of television's top shows. She says her job in life is "to walk on the beach."

On this particular Sunday morning, her beach was in Phoenix and I just happened to be there.

"This is the last day of your life." It was a set-up, of course. Something to put writing in the proper perspective, I guessed. Then she told us that, with that in mind, we should spend the next few minutes writing that book that was supposedly lurking inside.

I was furious!

My book was going to be a *business* book. How could this woman so callously grab my attention? She was telling me (or was I telling me?) that a business book wasn't important. She was telling me (or I was telling me!) that my book had to focus on bigger issues.

With only seconds left to write on this, my last day, I began:

"You're okay. I've always wanted you to know that. But in spite of my poor telling or perhaps because of it, you didn't hear. Or, if you heard, you didn't believe. So now with only three words left to my time—I love you."

I got it! A business book does not have to be dreary. It can be fun. My book was going to be human, soft, full of joy.

My anger had melted. I was bursting and couldn't wait to share. Not just the few ragged lines I had scribbled, but the discovery that it was perfectly okay to write in language that is as joyful as the very idea of Positively Outrageous Service.

When Viki asked, I volunteered. She hugged me. The lady sitting beside me hugged me. I was embarrassed, proud, and on fire to leave the room to start the book.

What transpired over the next few minutes, I cannot say. I stayed lost in thought until my seatmate nudged me. She passed a note. Why, that hadn't happened since genetics class in college!

"It's from the guy up front, the one with the beard," she whispered.

I opened the tan-colored paper that had been torn from the

hotel-provided note pad. A $20 bill fell out. In a clear, bold hand was written:

Scott—
> I want to buy a copy of your book.
>> Ray

"Ray" turned out to be Ray Pelletier, a speaker and now a friend, from Coral Gables, Florida.

I didn't walk out of the room that morning. I floated. I had been served positively outrageously. It was random and unexpected. Paying $20 for an unwritten book by an author you don't know couldn't be more out of proportion. And I was definitely invited to play. In fact, I was invited to write this book!

At Christmas, Viki sent the best card ever. Her handwritten message was:

Dear Scott,
> All best
> Joy and love,
> (It's your business)
>> Viki

TO BE CONTINUED . . .

About the Author

T. Scott Gross is America's expert on "everyday showmanship." He is a nationally recognized speaker/consultant to some of this nation's largest corporations and associations. Gross developed Positively Outrageous Service to explain how a few "contrarian businesses," including his own, are thriving and growing in the face of radical change and intense competition. He lives in Center Point, Texas, near San Antonio.

If you have a story of Positively Outrageous Service or P.O.S. Marketing that you would like to see included in future books, please write to:

T. Scott Gross
HCR 1, Box 561
Center Point, Texas 78010

Include your name, address, and telephone number so that you can be contacted if more details are required (and so that you can be properly acknowledged for your contribution).

Additional copies of *Positively Outrageous Service: New and Easy Ways to Win Customers for Life* may be ordered by sending a check for $14.95 (please add the following for postage and handling: $2.00 for the first copy, $1.00 for each added copy) to:

MasterMedia Limited

16 East 72nd Street
New York, NY 10021
(212) 260-5600
(800) 334-8232

T. Scott Gross is available for keynotes and seminars. Please contact MasterMedia's Speakers' Bureau for availability and fee arrangements. Call Tony Colao at (908) 359-1612.

Other MasterMedia Books

THE PREGNANCY AND MOTHERHOOD DIARY: Planning the First Year of Your Second Career, by Susan Schiffer Stautberg, is the first and only undated appointment diary that shows how to manage pregnancy and career. ($12.95 spiralbound)

CITIES OF OPPORTUNITY: Finding the Best Place to Work, Live and Prosper in the 1990's and Beyond, by Dr. John Tepper Marlin, explores the job and living options for the next decade and into the next century. This consumer guide and handbook, written by one of the world's experts on cities, selects and features forty-six American cities and metropolitan areas. ($13.95 paper, $24.95 cloth)

THE DOLLARS AND SENSE OF DIVORCE: The Financial Guide for Women, by Judith Briles, is the first book to combine practical tips on overcoming the legal hurdles with planning before, during, and after divorce. ($10.95 paper)

OUT THE ORGANIZATION: How Fast Could You Find a New Job?, by Madeleine and Robert Swain, is written for the millions of Americans whose jobs are no longer safe, whose companies are not loyal, and who face futures of uncertainty. It gives advice on finding a new job or starting your own business. ($11.95 paper, $17.95 cloth)

AGING PARENTS AND YOU: A Complete Handbook to Help You Help Your Elders Maintain a Healthy, Productive and Independent Life, by Eugenia Anderson-Ellis and Marsha Dryan, is a complete guide to providing care to aging relatives. It gives practical advice and resources to the adults who are helping their elders lead productive and independent lives. ($9.95 paper)

CRITICISM IN YOUR LIFE: How to Give It, How to Take It, How to Make It Work for You, by Dr. Deborah Bright, offers practical advice, in an upbeat, readable, and realistic fashion, for turning criticism into control. Charts and diagrams guide the reader into managing criticism from bosses, spouses, children, friends, neighbors, and in-laws. ($9.95 paper, $17.95 cloth)

BEYOND SUCCESS: How Volunteer Service Can Help You Begin Making a Life Instead of Just a Living, by John F. Raynolds III and Eleanor Raynolds, C.B.E., is a unique how-to book targeted to business and professional people considering volunteer work, senior citizens who wish to fill leisure time meaningfully, and students trying out various career options. The book is filled with interviews with celebrities, CEOs, and average citizens who talk about the benefits of service work. ($9.95 paper, $19.95 cloth)

MANAGING IT ALL: Time-Saving Ideas for Career, Family, Relationships and Self, by Beverly Benz Treuille and Susan Schiffer Stautberg, is written for women who are juggling careers and families. Over two hundred career women (ranging from a TV anchorwoman to an investment banker) were interviewed. The book contains many humorous anecdotes on saving time and improving the quality of life for self and family. ($9.95 paper)

REAL LIFE 101: (Almost) Surviving Your First Year Out of College, by Susan Kleinman, supplies welcome advice to those facing "real life" for the first time, focusing on work, money, health, and how to deal with freedom and responsibility. ($9.95 paper)

YOUR HEALTHY BODY, YOUR HEALTHY LIFE: How to Take Control of Your Medical Destiny, by Donald B. Louria, M.D., provides precise advice and strategies that will help you to live a long and healthy life. Learn also about nutrition, exercise, vitamins, and medication, as well as how to control risk factors for major diseases. ($12.95 paper)

THE CONFIDENCE FACTOR: How Self-Esteem Can Change Your Life, by Judith Briles, is based on a nationwide survey of six thousand men and woman. Briles explores why women so often feel a lack of self-confidence and have a poor opinion of themselves. She offers step-by-step advice on becoming the person you want to be. ($9.95 paper, $18.95 cloth)

THE SOLUTION TO POLLUTION: 101 Things You Can Do to Clean Up Your Environment, by Laurence Sombke, offers step-by-step techniques on how to conserve more energy, start a recycling center, choose biodegradable products, and proceed with individual environmental cleanup projects. ($7.95 paper)

TAKING CONTROL OF YOUR LIFE: The Secrets of Successful Enterprising Women, by Gail Blanke and Kathleen Walas, is based on the authors' professional experience with Avon Products' Women of Enterprise Awards, given each year to outstanding women entrepreneurs. The authors offer a specific plan to help you gain control over your life and include business tips and quizzes as well as beauty and lifestyle information. ($17.95 cloth)

SIDE-BY-SIDE STRATEGIES: How Two-Career Couples Can Thrive in the Nineties, by Jane Hershey Cuozzo and S. Diane Graham, describes how two-career couples can learn the difference between competing with a spouse and becoming a supportive Power Partner. Originally published in hardcover as *Power Partners.* ($10.95 paper)

DARE TO CONFRONT! How to Intervene When Someone You Care About Has an Alcohol or Drug Problem, by Bob Wright and Deborah George Wright, shows the reader how to use the step-by-step methods of professional interventionists to motivate drug-dependent people to accept the help they need. ($17.95 cloth)

WORK WITH ME! How to Make the Most of Office Support Staff, by Betsy Lazary, shows how to find, train, and nurture the "perfect" assistant and how best to utilize your support staff/professionals. ($9.95 paper)

MANN FOR ALL SEASONS: Wit and Wisdom from The Washington Post's *Judy Mann,* by Judy Mann, shows the columnist at her best as she writes about women, families, and the politics of the women's revolution. ($9.95 paper, $19.95 cloth)

THE SOLUTION TO POLLUTION IN THE WORKPLACE, by Laurence Sombke, Terry M. Robertson, and Elliot M. Kaplan, supplies employees with everything they need to know about cleaning up their workspace, including recycling, using energy efficiently, conserving water, buying recycled products and nontoxic supplies. ($9.95 paper)

THE ENVIRONMENTAL GARDENER: The Solution to Pollution for Lawns and Gardens, by Laurence Sombke, is a comprehensive how-to book that focuses on what each of us can do to protect our endangered plant life. A practical sourcebook and shopping guide. ($8.95 paper)

THE LOYALTY FACTOR: Building Trust in Today's Workplace, by Carol Kinsey Goman, Ph.D., offers techniques for restoring commitment and loyalty in the workplace. ($9.95 paper)

DARE TO CHANGE YOUR JOB—AND YOUR LIFE, by Carole Kanchier, Ph.D., provides a look at career growth and development throughout the life cycle. ($10.95 paper)

MISS AMERICA: In Pursuit of the Crown, by Ann-Marie Bivans, is an authorized guidebook to the Pageant, containing eyewitness accounts, complete historical data, and a realistic look at the trials and triumphs of potential Miss Americas. ($27.50 cloth)